Russian Studies in Philosophy

SUMMER 1995/VOL. 34, NO. 1

Cosmism and the Occult in Contemporary Russian Thought

Russian Studies in Philosophy (ISSN 1061–1967) is published quarterly by M. E. Sharpe, Inc., 80 Business Park Drive, Armonk, NY 10504. Subscription rates for U.S. institutions: one year, $381.00. For foreign institutions: one year, $421.00. Back issues of this journal are available at the subscription price effective on the date of the order. Price information on bulk orders or back volumes of the journal (to Vol.1, No.1) is available from M.E. Sharpe marketing director at 914-273-1800.

Second class postage paid at Armonk, NY and at additional mailing offices. Postmaster send address changes to *Russian Studies in Philosophy,* c/o M. E. Sharpe, Inc., 80 Business Park Drive, Armonk, NY 10504.

Editor's Introduction

JAMES P. SCANLAN

In the crowded firmament of postcommunist Russian philosophy, one constellation of ideas is particularly bright and active. These are the ideas associated with the quasi-scientific, quasi-spiritualistic world view called "Russian cosmism." The diverse complex of interests encompassed by this outlook ranges from empirically grounded biological, geological, and astrophysical studies to astrology and other excursions into the occult.

In its broadest, most abstract sense, the term 'cosmism' as employed in Russia today refers simply to a philosophy that takes the entire universe as its frame of reference and looks at earthly life in terms of the cosmic environment in which it is immersed. More concretely, the profile of cosmism in Russia has been shaped and colored since the late nineteenth century by the writings of a number of visionary but still controversial thinkers. They include the religiously minded librarian Nikolai Fedorov (1828–1903), who envisaged the physical resurrection of our ancestors as one aspect of gaining full human control over the cosmic forces of nature; the inventor Konstantin Tsiolkovskii (1857–1935), whose pioneering work in rocketry and the theory of space travel was inspired by a self-styled "cosmic philosophy"; the eminent earth scientist and Academician Vladimir Vernadskii (1863–1945), who believed in the eternity and omnipresence of living being ("animate matter") throughout the cosmos; and the artist-scientist Aleksandr Chizhevskii (1897–1964), who theorized about the impact of extraterrestrial forces and events on human life and society. It is the ideas of these and kindred thinkers, elaborating a "cosmic approach" in various and not always consistent directions, that are grouped together under the heading "Russian cosmism" by sympathetic Russian observers in the present day.

A sampling of these ideas is provided in the brief essay by Academician Vlail' Kaznacheev that opens this issue. Although formally a statement introducing the first issue of a new journal, *Russkaia mysl'* (Russian thought), Kaznacheev's essay exemplifies several characteristics of present-day Russian cosmism. First, of course, is the universalist orientation implicit in his references to the "planetary" character of Russian thought, to "spaceship

Planet Earth," and to mankind as "the only cosmoplanetary system." Second, Kaznacheev, a prominent scientist himself, invests "cosmic thinking" with the mantle of genuine science, albeit science of a "nontraditional" sort. Third, he is interested above all in the cosmos as an animate, even conscious reality; the connection of "animate matter" with "cosmic reason," he writes, is a conclusion not of fantasy but of science. Finally, like many contemporary devotees of Russian cosmism, he tends (far more than its historical originators did) to regard "cosmic consciousness" as a distinctively Russian ("Euro-Asiatic") intellectual contribution, and one, moreover, having immense significance not only for the future of Russia but for "planetary evolution" in general.

Gennadii Aksenov's highly sympathetic account of Vernadskii's life and thought in the second article makes clear the spiritual impulses and spiritualistic concepts behind the scientist's theory of "animate matter." In Aksenov's interpretation, Vernadskii's view of the primitive and pervasive character of life, according to which all mineral products in the universe are vestiges of or are created by living things, was a response to his essentially religious quest for cosmic unity—a quest in which dreams and other non-logical, intuitive states of consciousness were accorded equal legitimacy with empirical and rational analysis. By accepting "the mystery of illumination," Aksenov argues, Vernadskii was able not only to achieve an immediate grasp of the whole of reality but to live a "parallel" psychic life in which he could subjectively experience geological time. Although Aksenov shies from describing these experiences as mystical, they fit the classic accounts of mystical apprehension of "the oneness of being," and they suggest the degree to which cosmism is open to occult interpretations.

A far less sympathetic treatment of an "animate-universe" theory like Vernadskii's is presented in Nikolai Gavriushin's paper of Tsiolkovskii, the father of Russian rocket science. Tsiolkovskii shared Vernadskii's conviction of the vital character of matter, which he elaborated in directions that were taken also, as Gavriushin points out, by Madame Blavatsky and other theosophists (with whose works Tsiolkovskii was familiar); these included adopting the views that all matter is sensate and that the universe is a hierarchy of forms of consciousness. On the strength of these parallels Gavriushin does not hesitate to speak of "the deep connection between theosophic mysticism and cosmism." More than that, he links Tsiolkovskii's philosophy with a radical social utopianism comparable to Fourier's, and hence with social engineering of a potentially dangerous kind. He warns that in present-day Russia the "myth" of Tsiolkovskii's cosmic philosophy is contributing to a "technocratic pseudoreligiosity" that disregards genuine religious and humane values.

The last three articles in this issue were originally parts of a special section devoted to cosmism and related occult trends in a recent issue (1994, no. 2) of the journal *Voprosy filosofii*. As the (clearly skeptical) editors explained in a note, printed here at the beginning of the article "The Living Cosmos: Man Among the Forces of Earth and Heaven" by Vladimir Filatov, the current vogue of these trends in Russia suggested the need for an investigation of their origin and character. The articles are not simply exposés, however; each of them finds some positive value in the intellectual phenomena under investigation.

Filatov, in "The Living Cosmos," supplies the cosmic perception of the world with respectable historical credentials, by identifying it as the typical world perception of ancient times; even Plato and other sophisticated philosophers of classical antiquity, he argues, regarded the world as a "single organism suffused by life." Although spiritualized in the middle ages and then subverted by modern analytical science, the cosmic perception was not destroyed; it was merely marginalized, while its philosophical expression was continued by such thinkers as Goethe, Schelling, and the Russian cosmists. Filatov attributes the persistence of the cosmic perception to the universal human possession of mystical capacities, rooted in the right hemisphere of the brain. Because the rationalistic, technological environment of today creates a need for "more integral forms of spiritual experience," these is a place for cosmic perception in the modern intellectual economy. But in an abrupt caveat at the end of the article (reminiscent of qualifications added by Soviet authors to placate Marxist-Leninist censors), Filatov warns that such recourse to "cosmic consciousness" is in fact retrograde and that the *non*-cosmic perception of the world is more complex and richer.

Irina Beskova, in "The Nature of Transpersonal Experience," also ascribes an ancient pedigree to the conviction that man is at one with the cosmos, a conviction she sees as rooted in "archaic perception" characterized by immediacy, wholeness, and spontaneity; this primitive form of perception, she believes, is behind contemporary claims of memory of prenatal events, the transmigration of souls, and other transpersonal phenomena. Unlike Filatov, however, she does not appeal to mystical capacities, either historical or modern, to account for these phenomena. Rather, she argues that the present-day "experiences" on which these doctrines are based are the product of naturalistic mechanisms of information transfer from generation to generation, whereby our distant ancestors' naive, unanalytic perceptions are preserved and passed on through chains of parental influence, internalization, and memory. Interestingly, the authority on whose work she relies to develop her hypothesis is the American psychoanalytic theorist Eric Berne, author of *Games People Play*.

In his article on astrology, Boris Pruzhinin takes up a "cosmic" theory the popularity of which in Russia today goes far beyond the circle of those who have a philosophical interest in cosmism and the occult. Although acknowledging that the pretensions of astrology to the status of a science cannot fully be justified, Pruzhinin disagrees with those who reject astrology as a completely unscientific and fatalistic theory. He emphasizes the historical contribution of astrology in expanding our knowledge of the stars and planets, and he admits (somewhat in the spirit of William James's pragmatic assess- ment of human beliefs) that astrological convictions can have value as "one of the mechanisms of self-regulation of human activity." What is troubling about the revival of astrology in Russia today, Pruzhinin argues in conclu- sion, is not the content of astrological doctrine as such but its ideologization and possible misuse for purposes of political manipulation. We could say the same for cosmism in general, particularly when, paradoxically, the "cosmic" orientation is held to be a distinctive feature of the Russian mind and is thereby associated with the irrationalistic appeal of Russian national patriotism. (For further discussion of cosmism and its relation to Russian nationalism, see James P. Scanlan, ed., *Russian Thought after Communism: The Recovery of a Philosophical Heritage* [Armonk, NY, and London: M.E. Sharpe, 1994], pp. 26–28.)

V.P. KAZNACHEEV

Russian Thought

An Achievement of Humanity

1. Russian thought is a collective and symbolic concept. The intellect of any people on the planet Earth is great in its own way; nor can its contribution to the common planetary home of mankind be assessed on the basis of the generally accepted events of history. First, because these events in the history of mankind (as knowledge deepens, the true monuments are restored) are overestimated; second, because many of them are still beyond the bounds of knowledge and understanding. The true mechanisms of the evolution of mankind are still awaiting their Columbuses. The histories of the utilization of nature by social organisms, economics, natural science, culture, and religions are becoming increasingly disassociated; mankind, as the only cosmoplanetary system, remains in the world of hypotheses; pragmatic (very often tactical) aspirations (projects) supplant strategies of development and survival. The established priority of scientific and technical thought rejects empirical and *a priori* indicators. The experience of mankind's survival is condescendingly received or arrogantly ignored if it does not accord with the contemporary paradigms of science. This total, hidden scientific-cognitive actualism as regards how we see the world (the scientific picture of the world) was established as the highest level for the evaluation of national cultures in history and in modern times. The formula of civilized countries (of scientific and technical progress [STP])—"STP + Nature + Man"—is accepted as an ideal model for the world of the planet. Thus, for most Asian, African, and South American cultures, the contemporary civilizations of the developed countries are becoming a kind of sole ideal, the paths along which all the nations of the globe should move. The measure of this evaluation is the measure of STP, that is, of modern established science.

Russian text © 1992 by "Obshchestvennaia pol'za." "Russkaia mysl'—fenomen chelovechestva," *Russkaia mysl'*, 1992, no. 2, pp. 3–6.

Professor Vlail' Petrovich Kaznacheev is an Academician of the Russian Academy of Medical Sciences and the Academy of Natural Sciences of the Russian Federation.

The economic measure for the level of development of nations and countries is not equivalent to the levels of intellect, culture, humanism, and the ethics of national groupings.

The formula of development and of the models of evolution "Nature + Man + STP" or "Man + Nature + STP" requires of mankind other forms of mutual understanding, respect, and cooperation. The more crowded mankind becomes on the spaceship Planet Earth, the more important, the more weighty becomes the contribution of each national culture (each nation) and the more uniform becomes the standard for measuring the greatness of nations—each of them acquired its own greatness in history. The culture, lifestyle, experience, science, religion, and social and family-clan institutions of each nation are their unrepeatable self-expression, their unrepeatable and irreplaceable part of the phenomenon of mankind.

In developing the ideas of a single sphere of intellect, the pneumatosphere (P. Florenskii), the noosphere (V.I. Vernadskii), the universum (Teilhard de Chardin), one cannot accept a process of mere union, some impersonal globality, without understanding the value, without singling out the role of each historical "person," where person is understood to mean a national formation. The problems of the evolution of nations, their unification, their intellect, is above all a problem of their contemporary dynamics, in which natural-biological and cosmic-planetary evolution itself does not stop but is accelerated both qualitatively and quantitatively: the nature (biogenetic, intellectual) of man himself also changes and evolves. These new evolutionary processes are not homogeneous; they accelerate and are realized on the basis of past currents in the history (evolution) of nations, national formations, and their interactions. Although these problems are already being formulated in modern ethnology, the historical mission, the role of each nation in the dynamics of planetary evolution, remains no more than a hopeful prospect for natural science.

If we take modern scientific knowledge as representing 100 percent, the share of knowledge of the inert (nonliving) micro- and macrocosmos is about 95 percent, while the share of our knowledge of animate matter (V.I. Vernadskii) comprises merely 5 percent. Of this minimum, knowledge of the nature of man (the Phenomenon of Man) is less than 1 percent of all the world scientific knowledge of mankind. That is why there is currently no place either for animate matter or for man and his intellect in the scientific picture of the universe. After all, world models for survival according to the formula "STP + Nature + Man" draw their resources from the inert world. The more mankind "consumes" the planet's inert world for its own needs, the less knowledge remains about the true nature of man himself. The evolution of animate matter and of man is speeding up faster than the speed at which scientific knowledge about the actual essence of man, about humanity, about its cosmo-planetary significance, and about its place in the universe's infinitude is growing. Mankind, led by science, is playing its last Olympics on this global world arena: nature and the phenomenon of man and mankind are changing more rapidly. The science of man is lagging further and further behind along the raceway of survival, and the gap in the race toward a world of ruin is increasing irreversibly. In this race, each year at the end of the twentieth century is turning into seconds in the "clinical death" of animate matter and its extraterrestrial, mankind.

2. The history and culture of the Slavic-speaking peoples (above all in its planetary scale) is Euro-Asiatic. It was formed in the harsh natural expanses where the North played an essential role in the sphere of appropriation and survival. It is a Euro-Asiatic northern culture or a Eurasian culture with a large share of northern natural landscape.

The convergence of Slavic cultures with the national and natural cultures of Asia is a unique phenomenon; it is a mutual penetration. It includes the great migrations from Asia to Europe; it also includes the movement along northern and southern routes from Europe to Asia, its northern and southern limits. The natural, social, and political (economic) mechanisms of these interactions varied, but they produced a synthesis of culture and intellect and also altered family-clan and genetic mechanisms (processes of pan-mixing [panmiksiia]). Cultural flows from the west, south, and north of Europe, as well as the flows of Asiatic cultures, the cultures of Eastern and Southern Asia, were a direct part of these mechanisms.

Thus the formation of present-day Russia and its nations is a global phenomenon; in it is concentrated the base of its own national pedigree, the experience of European and Asiatic intellect, the elements of lifestyle, continuity of generations, the uses of nature, culture, religion, science, all the arts, and literature.

Most of all, these features found expression in the image of the Russian character: its lack of limits, its unboundedness, goodness, and patience; the predominance in it of altruism, self-sacrifice, and other-worldliness in the choice of life's principal, vital goals; further, a special attitude toward the earth, nature, and the human soul. The adoption and spread of the Greco-Christian Faith was no accident; the way to it was prepared by the whole of preceding history; religious tolerance and firmness in one's own faith are characteristics of this unifying spiritual principle.

Much has been said about the character traits of the Russian people [narod] in, for example, the studies of N.O. Losskii. However, it should be noted that over the four generations of the population of Russia (USSR) under the regime of the dictatorship, a considerable segment of the generations with the most vivid traits of Russian character was destroyed; the system of continuity of cultural and family traditions largely lost its significance. Some inevitable changes, a kind of settling not in the best direction took place in character traits. The strongest national traits were preserved as a substantially reduced (potential) natural and social possession. D.S. Likhachev identified these features in his recent work "On the National Character of Russians" [O natsional'nom kharaktere russkikh] (*Voprosy filosofii*, 1990, no. 4). He stressed that

> the striving of Russians toward liberty must be steered along the path of developing spiritual plurality [*mnozhestvennost'*] and spiritual freedom and of giving diverse creative opportunities to youth. . . . The striving of Russians to reach the ultimate limit in everything must be developed primarily in the spiritual domain. . . . Let the instinctive striving to give oneself up entirely to some holy cause, which has always so distinguished Russians, again take its worthy place and divert the Russian person from disfiguring patterns of thinking alike, acting alike, and submitting alike.

The nineteenth and the beginning of the twentieth centuries was a period of the greatest upsurge of the Russian intellect: of philosophy, sociology, art, literature, science (in the humanities and in the technical sphere); it was a kind of new era of enlightenment and encyclopedism. It is totally obvious that this was a social-societal, intellectual-cultural phenomenon, in which the political edifice merely abetted the intellectual explosion but was not itself its determining foundation. The aggregate of this explosion is the very phenomenon that today we can call Russian thought. Above all, it refers to the scale on which natural and social phenomena are evaluated—cosmism; next, it is a combination of scientific methods of cognition and *a priori* thought, and of the experience of the utilization of nature. It is the attempt to use the new knowledge of European science and culture but not to be transformed into an extension and imitation of Europe. Westernizing currents enriched Russian thought but never conquered it, and the same is true of the principal purely national priorities: Slavophilism also merely enriched but did not enslave Russian thought and the Russian intellect.

It is enough to recall the ideas and works of M.V. Lomonosov, D.I. Mendeleev, S.S. Podolinskii, V.I. Vernadskii, or of N.A. Umov, K.E. Tsiolkovskii, and A.L. Chizhevskii for all these cultural-historical characteristics to become obvious. The Euro-Asiatic phenomenon of Russian thought remains today the foundation of the renaissance of Russia as a whole. Political and economic dynamics today are drawing Russian thought and culture increasingly toward the pole of Westernism. Western ideals and the Western model of lifestyle, science, and culture are being imposed (this has already happened once before!) on Russia by someone's will. Some moderation is needed in all of this; Westernism cannot save the peoples [*narody*] and nations [*natsii*] of Russia, its intellect, its culture, or the economics of its survival.

If the nation lost more than half of its intellect on the operating table of world politics (1918–1990), the only possible path of its restoration and national development is A SPIRITUAL AND CULTURAL RENAISSANCE; not simply a restoration of past achievements but a further national development (in all the peoples of Russia) of its contemporary Euro-Asiatic intellect—the free movement of scientific and cultural thought in all spheres of the human and natural universe, and the creation of a fertile soil for the development of talent, of individual persons, of their innate aptitudes and their genius.

V.I. Vernadskii wrote that "among the preconditions for the contemporary revolution were free scientific ideas and scientific inquiry, its liberation to a significant degree from the pressure of religious, philosophical, and political structures and the creation within the social and state order of conditions favorable for free scientific thought."

Within the strata of Russia's scientific thought, the paths of such freedom have now matured in astrophysics, physics, and chemistry; marked out are paths of new discoveries forming a new vision of the entire scientific picture of the world, the macromicrocosm of the inert matter of the Universe, paths of the discovery of new sources of energy. Investigation of the nature of animate matter has uncovered new forms of its organization, and the hypothesis has been put forth about the plurality of forms of animate matter (protein-nucleic forms, field forms, and others) and their possible interaction. We have sufficient data about the cosmic-planetary mechanism for the appearance of rational forms of animate matter and the appearance of rational man on the planet as a special form of the living cosmos by way of the transformation of cerebral, nervous, and computer constructions of the CONDUCTIVE TYPE into computer systems of FIELD ORGANIZATION.

On the basis of such structures (intellectual Earth-spots), adaptation has brought about the creation of semantic and linguistic fields as a consequent secondary planetary system of adaptation.

Anthropocentism and anthropocosmism are still holding back the further development of a new cosmogony, and the "intellectual black hole" (see above) is growing wider and wider within the semantic mechanisms of the modern intellect. Hopes for the introduction of computer systems into social-societal, industrial, and everyday practice and for the creation of a computer wave of civilization will make the ultimate fatalism of this "black hole" irreversible. Further, it is becoming more and more obvious that the bioenergetic mechanisms of animate matter based on oxidizing processes are the simplest (but not the only) energy "machine" of protein-nucleic forms of life. Field (holographic) organizations have other energy sources and probably other spatio-temporal dimensions (continuums)—the reference is to a "cold biothermoiad" [*kholodnyi biotermoiad*]. The old writings of Louis Kervran, contemporary data, and our investigations of the correlations between stable carbon isotopes (C_{12} and C_{13}) in the cells of people of different ages confirm the probability of the transmutation of elements in biosystems. According to calculations, processes of transmutation of elements require very high sources of energy, approaching the level of the known nuclear reactors. The problems of paleopsychology and their relevance to the modern world of spirituality appear in a new light.

Mankind is striving to find a way of survival; the European model ("STP + Nature + Man") is by no means the only model and cannot be applied on a global scale. The prospects of several models of cooperation among peoples and states and later their integration, their coordination at the level of the "living earth," of Gaia, the living cosmos, the interaction of different intellectual (rational) forms of animate matter existing independently today on the planet Earth, and their interaction with cosmic reason—these are not fantastic but scientific-cultural, realistic prospects of survival. It is to these paths of Russian thought that its own most important, irreplaceable role has been devoted and will be devoted in a universal, international unity. This historical national drama that has taken place in Russia will probably become a new driving force for the resurrection of the peoples of Russia. This is possible only on the basis of its unique sociohistorical, psychological, and natural-biological, truly natural character. Everything that can promote this process is worthy of respect and support. Building the temple of man on a new level in the world community is in fact the historical realization of the Russian idea, of the lofty global humanity of Russian thought. The thoughtful reader will understand that the author has attempted in the foregoing to synthesize as far as his knowledge permits the extremely great legacy of our culture and science. I have intentionally not named the predecessors and authors of these ideas. That is impossible, and references to the individual works of the authors of Russian encyclopedism would be insufficiently correct and objective, since many names still remain buried under the ruins of the bloody dictatorial system: their restoration, the restoration of the true events of our national history, is also a coming movement of our Russian thought.

3. The restoration of our Russian traditions of enlightenment is the most important cause today. The initiative of the publishers of this journal does not signify under the title *Russkaia mysl'* that it is a continuation of the

well-known literary and political publication *Russkaia mysl'* founded by
V.M. Lavrov in Moscow (1880–1918) and then resurrected outside Russia
by P.B. Struve (Sofia, Prague, Paris). The most outstanding philosophical
scholars, literati, critics, journalists, and historians participated in that journal.
The historical and cultural role of those publications is great, and their
evaluation requires a special study. What V.G. Rodionov has succeeded in
doing at present—the preparation and publication of two volumes of the
journal (1991–92) under the title *Russkaia mysl'*—has a substantively
different foundation. It is a kind of interesting test of one of the paths of
free illumination of the scientific thought of the past and the present and
above all of nontraditional scientific currents of ideas and research. There
are successes and shortcomings in this regard. It is our task not to judge the
journal but to support its creative initiative and the efforts of its editor and
contributors in every way. This is one of the first swallows of the "spring of
the rebirth" of Russia. One would like to believe that its harbingers will feel
warm in their Motherland. But now it is necessary to congratulate all of us
on the fact that a new generation of enlighteners is gathering strength in
Russia. Success to them in forging the new roads of the future!

G.P. AKSENOV

The Scientific Solitude of Vernadskii

The title of this article will perhaps seem excessively contentious to the reader. What solitude of Vladimir Ivanovich Vernadskii, he might ask, if he has even the slightest familiarity with the scientist's biography?

Truly, Vernadskii was neither a medieval anchorite monk nor a modern Faust. He was shaped by and circulated his entire life in a normal academic environment. He received a systematic education at St. Petersburg University, at a time, moreover, when the best Russian scientists were assembled within its walls. He exhibited a talent as a researcher early. He was groomed by Dokuchaev and retained to prepare for the calling of professor. He defended his candidate's thesis, then his master's and doctoral dissertations, and was appointed an Academician.

He trained a great many students in his twenty-five years of teaching. His ideas are not only set down in texts but have been implemented in the form of institutes, laboratories, expeditions, and libraries. He was a rector, a president, a director, and a member of numerous scientific societies, and he associated very actively, both orally and in writing, with Russian and foreign colleagues.

His life outside science also took place among people. He was surrounded by friends, comrades-in-arms, and like-minded people from childhood to a ripe old age. He did much for Russia as educator, essayist, and politician. The extent of his work for the state in organizing science and knowledge is only now becoming truly revealed.

His house on Durnovskii Lane in Moscow received visitors every day, as is clear from recently published diaries for 1938.[1] Business partners, aging peers, budding talents, and the widows of scientists would visit, sensing there moral backing and support. As has now become clear, Vernadskii resisted Stalin's terror both actively and passively.[2]

Nor can one fail to mention his harmonious family life with Natal′ia

Russian text © 1993 by "Nauka" Publishers and "Voprosy filosofii." "O nauchnom odinochestve Vernadskogo," *Voprosy filosofii*, 1993, no. 6, pp. 74–87. A publication of the Institute of Philosophy, Russian Academy of Sciences.

Gennadii Petrovich Aksenov is a historian and a member of the Journalists' Union.

Egorovna (née Staritskaia)—fifty-six years "together in soul and thought," as he used to say—and also with his loving children.

Finally, there is his enviable posthumous scientific fate. His achievements in geochemistry, mineralogy, radiology, crystallography, soil science, and other fields have long since left the personal domain and have become a part of course material and technology. His theory of the biosphere is being developed quite vigorously.[3] His noosphere ideas are a permanent part of philosophical language.

All this is so.

Yet I shall still maintain that in Vernadskii's creative life there is an uninhabited island, an unfathomed sphere that insistently compels intellectual attention. We do not yet know, but we have a vague sense, that Vernadskii is not simply a great professional. His spiritual quest, the innermost metaphysical depth of his at times not very clear statements, casts a spell on us. There is some inner core where strands from all the sciences, from his own person, and from his life converge.

Nor is this domain hidden or coded—Vernadskii is published virtually in his entirety, leaving mostly personal archival material. On the contrary, it resonates on each page he wrote and shines through every definition. Not only his pure science but his actions are pervaded by its spirit, for he, as a truly Russian intellectual, did not separate his work from his life.

The source [*prichina*] of Vernadskii's "Cosmos" is a sense of the eternity of life and consciousness, a quest for the unity and the integrity of the world. He applied all his powerful intellect and his utterly incredible encyclopedic erudition to the task of demonstrating the nonrandomness of life and its cosmic character. For the time being his theory remains in the personal form in which he conceived it, as a kind of amalgam of precise observation and calculation, philosophical reflection and religious feeling—in that synthetic unity that has no name other than the name of its creator itself.

We read his lines and do not understand the meaning contained in them. Vernadskii is just as alone fifty years after his death as he was in life.

The mystery of the individual person

We shall begin with a remarkable event that happened to the scientist in February–March of 1920 in the Crimea. He left testimony about it that can in no way be classified as sober, rational scientific language.

True, the times themselves were quite irrational. The powerful intrusion of barbarism upended and crushed all social strata. The existing order, which took centuries to establish, was liquidated in an instant. The ground fell away from under one's feet.

But Vernadskii was sustained by inner work, by a certain conjecture. As early as 1908, he was struck by a seditious thought. He took a separate piece of paper and wrote roughly the following: If from a geochemical viewpoint one can establish that animate matter is a necessary stage in the cycle of chemical elements, then one must acknowledge that the quantity of the living on Earth is constant. Life is a planetary constant. Thus, at the periphery of his consciousness some sort of strange "law of the conservation of quantity" of life began to glimmer.

And the more he read, observed, and thought over the next twelve years, the more firmly did it become established in his consciousness that the concept of animate matter was by no means a particular one; it was in some unfathomable way a part of the structure of the entire Cosmos. A discovery of the first order had been vouchsafed him, a kind of Mayerian principle of the conservation of energy.

The words 'animate matter' [*zhivoe veshchestvo*] became key. He thought about them persistently throughout all the chaotic years of war and revolution, stealing hours here, minutes there. In 1916, he began to sketch "Thoughts About Animate Matter," without any form, simply notes, because he did not know whether he would survive the fortuities of the times.

Two weeks after October 1917, Vernadskii, as a member of the Provisional Government meeting clandestinely, signed two extremely important documents: an appeal to the citizens of Russia in which the Bolsheviks were declared usurpers, and a decree about convening a Constituent Assembly; he thereby put himself in an illegal situation. He was forced to go into hiding and flee the capital.

A year and a half later, he was living in the ephemeral Ukrainian state, where he created the Academy of Sciences and the National Library that now bears his name. After the collapse of the Volunteer Army, which had abandoned Kiev, he wandered about behind the White forces' lines for two months. This was followed in January 1920 by a move to the Crimea, on the hellish steamship the Great Queen Xenia, overflowing with typhus patients, from Novorossiisk to Yalta. Here, on the Bakunin estate Gornaia Shchel' he was reunited with his family and could briefly catch his breath.

It seemed that all was lost. He did not know when normal scientific work would resume. There was no information about the two academies, about his laboratories on Vasil'evskii Island, or about his apartment.

Then came illness—typhoid fever. Here are the last lines he wrote when already in bed with a fever: "I understand Condorcet, when before his death he wrote his *Esquisse* in exile, without books. He had the same thought as I: if I do not now write my 'thoughts about animate matter,' it will be a long time yet before this idea is born again, and perhaps never in this form. Could I be wrong in evaluating their significance and novelty in the history of human thought?"[4]

As a drowning man convulsively takes his last gasps of air, his mind clung to something with the name "animate matter" and prevented the waters of nonbeing from closing over his head. He and those close to him were convinced that he was saved by scientific thinking. As soon as his mind cleared, Vernadskii dictated to Natal'ia Egorovna the methodology of experiments and the instrumental set-up for the study of organisms. Like Archimedes, he tried above all to save the sketches.

A few days later, when he improved, he began to write on his own and tried to express something unprecedented that had come over him during his illness. In a strange state, it seemed to him that he was living through his entire life from the present moment up to his death. All of the images of that life appeared so clearly and visibly before him that he even perceived sounds, heard conversations, and sensed odors. He saw himself going off to England, achieving huge scientific success, gaining a name for himself, and creating a large international institute for animate matter in America. Thus transpired a kind of real–unreal parallel life.[5]

Here we are touching upon that mystery of personality and creativity that many spirited and talented people have experienced—the mystery of illumination, of insight, of seemingly chance discoveries, of solutions to the most difficult problems that come to one in a dream, and so forth. Vernadskii's burst of creativity continued for three weeks. By all appearances, an entire new system of natural science was created, in its totality. Is such a thing possible?

Vernadskii thought both about his own experience and about other discoveries made via the seemingly nonlogical path of insight and intuition. He suspected that there was no mysticism in it. A second reality of psychic life, a reality of which we are not aware, has a different physical nature, for which velocities beyond the speed of light are characteristic. He confided these thoughts to his diary, where he constructed the following speculation: in the macroworld, the world of gravity, ordinary velocities operate; in the microworld, velocities of the speed of light; and in the world of the action of thought, speeds beyond the speed of light.[6]

If one attempts to explain the phenomenon rationally and considers, for example, time to be proportional to events of a specific class, one can assume that in his mental effort on the threshold of death Vernadskii really did experience a "parallel" life since, in terms of saturation with events of mental activity (and it is such activity that is a scientist's mode of existence), three weeks of thought undistracted by anything is equal, truly equal, to the twenty-five years of his remaining, chronologically measured life.

This internal, spontaneously experienced time is the subject of the meditations of Henri Bergson, who is philosophically the closest to Vernadskii. In Bergson's view, an individual's authentic, real life takes place intuitively. A person's own reflection, or that of others thinking about him—the awareness of the path already traveled—only gives shape to what has already been achieved, done, or gone through in accordance with specific rules in another time regime. Cognition of truth is a more complicated process than we think. It consists in not the contemplation but the experience of truth, its duration over time—not an ordinary time but an ultrafast regime involving the stretching out of minutes. When cognizing, reason does not observe; it forgets itself and participates, acts, organizing the time and space of the "parallel world." That is why Bergson's definition of man, *Homo faber* (Man Who Acts [*Chelovek Deistvuiushchii*]), refers to the inner life of the individual and not to ordinary objective reality.[7]

Of course, what absorbed Vernadskii during these three weeks, by all appearances, was action. What he later wrote is merely his recognition, his recollection of truth he experienced, his shaping of knowledge already achieved and residing in some compact form in the depths of internal connections.

Thus in his dialogue *Meno*, Plato has Socrates say that all of our most important knowledge is recollection, not the reflection of the external world. We receive everything in finished form from our immortal soul. Learning is only the search for the best way to force the soul to speak.

Perhaps we are indeed only remembering the whole time, if we only consider that the experiencing of truth took place at some earlier time, unconsciously, without witnesses, and then later, during the course of our lives, we draw on the results of hidden acts. In the desire to penetrate into the innermost sources, we consciously strive to fall into some internal rhythm, into a resonance, to "retrieve" what is contained in the subconscious. Socrates had his reasons when he used the example of frenzied priests, the Corybantes, who would fall into a trance and then begin to prophesy in beautiful images.

A scientist probably gets into his inner mood when he is doing the work he loves, that is, when he is engaged in observation or experiment. So it was with Vernadskii. In 1897, while on an excursion to southern Germany and observing the volcanic landscape around the Laacher See, he wrote the following about what he was feeling:

> When you walk briskly around a beautiful place, pictures of the past rush through your mind, sometimes astonishingly clearly but always instantaneously. Often they are so fast that they are *unconscious* [my emphasis—G.A.].

What remains is only an impression that they were there, a feeling or a memory of intense delight, but they themselves were not noticed by consciousness. Especially now, when I am trying to capture not a picture of a surface but a deeper property, chemical processes, thought operates pictorially in that manner.

During this time I think through many things. And the most diverse things come to mind, things that seemingly have no relation at all to the picture of the nature of this locality, to scientific observation, or to reflections upon seeing it.

But for me it is absolutely clear that it is precisely all these things that are interconnected, since scientific observation and reflection are the fullest and clearest manifestation of my spirit, and during this time "consciousness" is at its highest level of intensity.[8]

He lived through centuries as he pondered the geochemical processes that had created the volcanic landscape around the lake—geological centuries in ordinary minutes.

The history of culture is replete with such poetic, philosophical, and religious mysticism [*vizionerstvo*]. When a person has a moment of inspiration, a moment of love or passionate repentance, religious enthusiasm or moral insight, he finds the meaning of his own existence. At such moments, the Whole is embraced—not gradually, as from books, but immediately. An inner reality is sensed as the presence of some spiritual force, which one joins, or, put better, which joins man to itself. A person is no longer self-willed. He is seized by a feeling of absolute fearlessness. All doubts are left behind. His life is resolved.

Science is regarded as a more sober affair than other forms of creativity. But that depends on what kind of science, on what its scope is. Vernadskii writes that in his "parallel" life it turns out that he even composed aphorisms and spiritual hymns in honor of this unknown force: "In one of my thoughts, it seemed to me that in my experiences I touched very deeply on the explanation of life and the creativity associated with it, as a fusion with the Eternal Spirit, in which are formed or which is formed out of such strivings toward the search for truth on the part of the human consciousnesses, including my own."[9]

But the feeling of being chosen does not elicit pride. A person understands that he has been selected not for rest but for activity. Only now does his work cease to be a craft and become creative, for it is illuminated by the meaning of the Whole. And the scope of the activity has no significance. A person finds himself in a place where no one envies anyone and no one blocks anyone's path. Everyone must become aware only of his own unique and irreproducible way of connecting to the Whole, in accordance with his own knowledge and character. The traits of the individual person become traits of the structure of the Whole, of Nature. Everyone is given a tool to fit his hand and a tree to fit his stature. Man coincides with his calling.

For some reason he remembered the forgotten naturalists of the early nineteenth century—[Robert] Moffat, [John William] Colenso, [Sir James] Hector—who worked in South Africa and Polynesia and who were not only natural scientists but also missionaries. Vernadskii speculated about why they had appeared. Christian naturalists are distinguished by their consciousness of the divine nature of Creation and the sense of moral responsibility it engendered for coming up with an accurate, nondistorting cognition and description of nature. Their works are striking for their attention to the smallest details, for leaving out nothing essential, for leaving out nothing at all. The task of the scientist is not to divide things into what is important and what is secondary but accurately to record everything without presuming to decide what is important. Observation and description thus require the highest level of professionalism. Thus, says Vernadskii, the religious foundation of the exact natural sciences emerges. To confuse the languages is to weaken both religion and science.[10]

The scientist's religiosity gives him an impulse to activity that is very closely linked to his own sense of being chosen, of "assignment" to a particular place. No one after him will do this work. He is the last in some series. Henceforth he has no personal affairs; he has a personal way of realizing a common cause.

"I began to understand clearly," Vernadskii sums up, "that I was condemned to tell humanity something new with the theory of animate matter that I am creating and that is my calling, my duty, imposed upon me, which I must implement—like a prophet, who senses within himself a voice calling him to activity. I felt within myself Socrates's demon."[11]

Now we must examine whether the "Crimean vision" was realized. Was Vernadskii able to "retrieve" from his subconscious a new theory in which life, animate matter, and the individual person were scientifically recognized parts of the cosmos?

Is the Cosmos possible without life?

Exactly one year later, in 1921, the scientist returned to Russia. Having by that time been appointed rector of Tavricheskii University, he attempted to make it into an autonomous institution, but once again the Bolsheviks caught up with him. He left the ranks of rectors and accomplished a no less fantastic journey than the one the year before, across the entire country, from the Black Sea to the Barents Sea.

He traveled through southern Ukraine, where he had taken field trips with Dokuchaev, through the locales of his childhood, staying in both capitals, associating with people of the most diverse strata, and even ending up in prison. In Petrograd he was arrested, but he was released on Lenin's decision and immediately left for the biological station near Murmansk.

Vernadskii was greatly shaken by what he had seen and doubted even whether it was possible to restore culture in this country. Would not it have been better, that inner voice suggested, to leave for England? In Moscow, where he gave a report to his colleagues, he nonetheless wrote: "Sometimes a sense of certainty is arising that I shall do a lot. I believe in what I am destined for. I clearly realize that in not going to London and remaining here I perhaps have altered the form of my achievement, but the basic idea remains unchanged—the creation of an Institute for the Study of Animate (or Geochemical?) Matter. And maybe ultimately I shall go to America?"[12] In the end, a "feeling of Russia" won out.

In May 1921 he gave a lecture at the Petrograd House of Writers with the characteristic title "The Beginning and the Eternity of Life" [Nachalo i vechnost' zhizni]. It was the first presentation of his idea.

For the first time he spoke publicly about the primitive character [neproiskhozhdenie] of life. All empirical biological facts testify to the fact that life is passed on only by life. No cases have been found of the self-inception of life out of the earth's inert material. Similarly unproven are archaeogenesis—the sudden origination of life at a moment in antiquity, during the pregeological periods of the Earth—or heterogenesis—the beginning of life in some hybrid way. These hypotheses, said Vernadskii, must be left to philosophy, religion, and art; science must stay on the solid ground of facts, not theories.

In the seventeenth century, the Florentine physician Francesco Redi formulated the following principle: "All that is living comes only from the living!" There are millions of confirmations of this, and not one refutation. But the inertia of thought is powerful. The human mind stubbornly clings to the construct of a genesis, a coming into being, and an inception.

Such a "natural" orientation of consciousness is in fact a presumption of myth, an archetype of thinking. The idea of a beginning means adding theological language to the language of science, since the concept of beginning and end of being came from Judeo-Christian escatology and spread throughout the entire European world. In other religions, for example, in the Hindu religion, the idea of a beginning is absent.

Science must go beyond a tradition that does not correspond to the facts. What seems "strange" is quite simple in science. "For European scientific thought we long ago discarded the idea of the logical necessity of posing the question of a beginning in regard to other matters, associated, for example, with matter, energy, or the ether. For them we have accepted infinity in time. We will probably also accept the same lack of beginning for life, for animate matter in the form of organisms, and we will accept also the lack of a beginning of the world."[13] Indeed, we do not ask when electricity, for example, or gravity arose. Without worrying about the incomprehensible, without worrying about the mind's bent to explain everything without fail, to reduce everything to intelligibility, we must accept the obvious: What is valid for today's Earth was valid also for its pregeological and cosmic periods. And it is valid for the whole Universe. Life is eternal, concludes Vernadskii.

He printed his lectures as a separate brochure but received no responses to his idea, if, of course, one disregards the stupid accusations of vitalism. The typical Soviet "criticism" began.

This was the peak decade of his life, beginning with the *Thoughts on Animate Matter* and ending with a year's work of the Institute of Animate Matter in France. Only the Institute consisted of him alone.

While he was living in France and trying without success to interest wealthy organizations, as, for example, the Carnegie Institute, in his ideas, Vernadskii suddenly received a gift of fate. A committee of French scientists who administered a fund established by Rosenthal, the "pearl king," to encourage scientific research gave him its maximum donation of 40,000 francs. He was able to live for a whole year without worrying about earning a livelihood and was even able to pay for the chemical analyses of animate matter he needed. That is how the "Institute," nurtured in his dreams, was formed.

Vernadskii abandoned all other matters. At that time he was even expelled from his Academy because he did not wish to return (they did not accept the argument that he wanted to finish his "life's work"). But Vernadskii had staked everything on one card. Again he left for his "island Crimea."

In the summer of 1924, he and Natal'ia Egorovna went to Brittany and rented a small house "at the edge of the waves and the waters" (as in his vision, too, the Institute was situated on the shore of the Atlantic Ocean). For the winter he moved to the small town of Bourg-la-Reine near Paris.[14]

Neither earlier nor later did Vernadskii experience such freedom of spirit and such intellectual élan. He spent a whole year totally absorbed in his work. Analytical chemists whom he knew furnished him with the necessary data on the elementary chemical composition of certain common, widely distributed organisms, and he sometimes spent whole days doing computations. He devised his formulas for the proliferation of animate matter, and he calculated the speed at which it occupies space and the pace at which it grows in weight and size. He obtained figures that captivate the imagination: one bacterium in one day of proliferation is theoretically capable of growing to a mass equal to that of the globe: its speed of proliferation is equal to the speed of sound.

Let us now look at the results of the decade in a logical, abbreviated, and simplified summation. Let us straighten a bit the historical path that Vernadskii traversed. The biogeochemistry and the theory about the biosphere that he created in those years do not in themselves prove the idea that life is eternal, although they do lead us in that direction.

The triune science of biogeochemistry provides the notion that life has existed forever on the planet, demonstrating the constancy of the chemical environment on its surface and the link between biological evolution (or, simply, life) and geological history. In particular, it is based on a principle of bio-actualism. If the biosphere today determines the conditions and character of chemical processes and the movement of masses of matter and energy on the planet, there are no grounds to assume that it was otherwise in the geological past. Conceptions of the evolution of life founder on the obvious but mistaken idea that life had a beginning or at least that it can be reduced to simple, primitive forms.

Primitive does not mean powerless but rather even the opposite. The power of the biosphere does not diminish the further one goes back into the past.

Moreover, there is also a nonevolving part of the biosphere, the bacteria S.N. Vinogradov discovered, which proved to be a second principal form of life, the prokaryotes [*prokarioty*]. They are the same today as they were billions of years ago. Hence one can say that the entire geological machine starts in the biosphere. All mineral products either consist of vestiges of living things or were "made" by them, especially bacteria and protozoa. The same may be said about all sedimentary rock. Animate matter transforms the energy of solar radiation into the energy of chemical bonds of inert matter, which for a long period, sometimes millions of years, remains stored in the bowels of the earth, where it is metamorphosed and reduced to magma under the effects of radioactive decay, pressure, and temperature; and if later it is forced out to the surface, it is once more subjected to a new cycle of crushing and weathering. The latter process is not mechanical but biogeochemical.

Clearly, the animate is a law-governed participant in this cycle and, what is more, is its initiator. Just as a circus horseman standing in the middle of the ring urges on the circling horse, so does animate matter in one place, in the surface layer of the biosphere, communicate an impulse of energy to inert matter, which then moves, drawn by its own forces—geological, tectonic, volcanic, radioactive, and so forth.

But it is difficult to be clear about the laws of animate matter at the level of the biosphere because of the great variety of its relations and processes. Vernadskii gradually came to concentrate on the more fundamental level of the interaction between animate and inanimate matter—on the atomic level. There are not thousands of atoms (isotopes), as there are thousands of minerals, rocks, and crystals, but only about 150 of them.

However, in interpreting even these magnificent geochemical laws, it is not unreasonable that we should declare that they are local and unique in the world because only one instance of the biosphere is known to us. Even supposing that life truly is the source from which all structures of the earth's crust and all differentiation and movement of elements receive energy, why should it be eternal? It simply invaded a lifeless cold planet and altered its entire surface environment.

How did life on earth appear? There are three conceivable answers, disregarding supernatural ones. First: life arose of itself as the result of a favorable confluence of circumstances. Second: life, having arisen somewhere, was then carried with the cosmic dust and meteorites in the form of spores and cysts (which, as we know, are capable of enduring for an indefinitely long period, perhaps billions of years, even in a vacuum and in the cold) and, encountering a favorable environment, burst into luxuriant bloom. The third answer: life has always been, and there was no beginning. From an atomic-molecular, geochemical, and biospheric perspective, all three answers seem equally hypothetical and in principle even unneeded. The revolutionary essence of the most incomprehensible of them, the third, is not recognized.

Vernadskii understood this himself. The logic of thought led him to the necessity of examining the most fundamental level—the level of space and time.

He concentrated not on the evolution of life but on its constancy and the unchanging nature of its manifestations. It has existed for billions of years. But what gives it such stability in the face of the incredible number of chance events in the nonliving world? "What we have here is a manifestation of deeper properties of matter or, more accurately, a form of its manifestation that is different from the properties of atoms and isotopes, different from physical-chemical properties in general. A plausible working hypothesis to investigate is that the bodies of living organisms are determined in their fundamentals by a geometric state of the space they occupy that is different from the Euclidian space of inert natural bodies in the biosphere."[15]

What kind of a geometry would this bē?

We know that the properties of any chemical or biological combination of molecules depend not only and not so much on elementary structure as on the way the atoms are arranged in the molecule. Here it would be appropriate to speak of the formation by animate matter of its own proper space.

Animate matter does not recognize cubes, squares, spheres, and other symmetrical figures in its crystalline structure. As a rule, it is structured by flowing lines, drops, curves, spirals—in other words, by asymmetric figures, and that at every level, from the molecule to the organism. But even the most irregular figure has a kind of symmetry. This is the symmetry of the whole, not a part of it—a mirror symmetry, the reflection of the entire figure in a mirror. Any molecule or set of molecules may be built of the same particles, but inversely. By the laws of symmetry, only two ways to construct it are admissible, left and right. No other figures opposite to the given one exist in nature. They are called isomers.

Now begins what is most important. By all the laws of physics and chemistry, the quantity of right and left matter should be the same. For example, we will synthesize some chemical compound in the laboratory, and it will decompose into two parts mirroring one another, a right and a left. This will be their racemic mixture. The percentage proportion of isomers depends on the quantity of matter. First, let us assume, there are seventy left isomers for every thirty right isomers, then sixty and forty, then fifty and fifty, and at this ratio the chemistry comes to a full stop forever, however much matter we still make. The more syntheses, the closer we come to a uniform distribution. These are the same laws as in throwing dice. The law of large numbers.

This result agrees with all the fundamental principles of nature and, above all, with the second law of thermodynamics, which requires an even distribution, in any system of anything at all, of temperature, chemical concentration, types of crystals, colors, and so forth.

Animate matter wants to be the fundamental of fundamentals. With millions and billions of syntheses of its irregular and flowing figures, it forms matter in only one spatial variety. Not 30 to 70 and not 10 to 90 but 100 percent of only one, either left or right matter. All living protein without exception is only left matter, and all glucose is only right matter. There are no others.

Louis Pasteur discovered this phenomenon and called it dissymmetry, that is, a kind of complemented and deepened asymmetry. And incidentally he considered it, rather than what he was famous for—pasteurization or the pathogen of rabies—to be the principal discovery of his life. He quite rightly thought that he had here come upon a universal, cosmic riddle that called into question everything in the natural world. From that time onward the mystery never subsided but, on the contrary, became as much a riddle as life itself. How, in what way, physicists and chemists asked, did animate matter "go astray" and switch from racemic (right–left) synthesis to dissymmetric synthesis? If life came about on Earth, where there were only racemic syntheses, then how did life transform them and become chirally (in the language of physics) pure? Perhaps Earth turned in its orbit and ran backwards? Or it began to rotate in the other direction? One has to admit His Majesty, chance.

Vernadskii saw nothing enigmatic in dissymmetry. Life did not at one time switch to dissymmetric synthesis, because it had always been engaged in it. Life was, is, and will be dissymmetric. The latter must be understood as the basic property of its spatial structure.[16] It holds at every structural level of the living organism and even in the functions of organs. DNA is always twisted to the left, just as the shells of mollusks are always one-sided. The number of left-handers is always unequal [to the number of right-handers]—16 in 100—and the functions of the hemispheres of the human brain, which externally differ in no respect, are nonidentical.

It is not difficult to see that dissymmetry is a second, reverse side of irreversibility, itself a temporal property. Vernadskii demonstrated that they were inseparably connected. To be living means to be dissymmetric and irreversible.

There are many reversible processes in the world. For example, one and the same or functionally equivalent minerals are formed in completely different geological epochs. Any chemical or mineral complex that has aged in the bowels of the earth's crust is ground down to "year zero" once it falls into the embrace of the eternally youthful biosphere and is again set out to age as sedimentary rock. And what are the "different geological epochs"? How do they differ? They all differ from one another in the composition and structure of the rocks. But the clearest identifying feature is the dissimilarity and unrepeatability of the animal and plant world of one epoch compared with another. The biota of the Cambrian period are unrecognizable compared with the biota of the Triassic period or of our Cenozoic era. Thus the eternally young biosphere, in contrast to recurrent rock, never returns to its previous state.

And not only the biosphere. The same takes place with a biocoenosis, a population of organisms, a discrete individual, or a cell. Animate matter is inherently directed from the past to the future, which as far as it is concerned means that two cells will never under any conditions fuse into one. They will only each divide into two. We always observe unfolding, developing, and differentiation and never involution, degradation, and simplification.

The irreversibility of what is living poses in full the question of time, for, Vernadskii observes,

> nowhere in the nature around us does *time* move to the same degree and with such a degree of organization as in animate matter. The great service of the French philosopher and biologist Henri Bergson was that he more clearly and deeply insisted on the importance of time for living organisms compared with inert natural bodies.
>
> At the basis of phenomena of symmetry in animate matter, time appears in a form and with a significance not present in inert bodies and in the phenomena of the biosphere. It seems to me that here what is clearly apparent at the basis of geometric notions is not so much space as some new, more complicated concept that has entered into the natural scientist's understanding in the twentieth century, the concept of *space–time, different from space and different from time.*
>
> Animate matter is so far the only case on our planet in which space–time and not space is tangibly manifested in the nature surrounding the naturalist. This space–time is not the concept of space–time in which time is the fourth dimension of space, that is, the space of mathematicians (Paladge, Minkowski), nor is it the space–time of physicists and astronomers, which is the space–time of Einstein.[17]

Thus we have come to where Vernadskii traveled with such difficulty and puzzlement throughout his entire life—to the central point of his conception. It is simple, hence difficult to comprehend, and it consists in an approach to space and time. Vernadskii did not consider these categories to be universal, as philosophy has become accustomed to doing, because for him they are not philosophical categories but facts of nature. And they belong not to all of reality but only to animate matter. "The only case so far on our planet . . ." Only animate matter has the properties of irreversibility and dissymmetry, the most important qualities of time and space.

Vernadskii called time vital or biological time and devoted a whole series of works to it, and even a book with that title, begun but not finished.[18]

The nonuniversality of time suggests the simple idea of the cause of time, its source. Time "forms" in animate matter. Consequently, it loses all its mysteriousness and becomes an ordinary property of animate matter like heredity, which once also seemed to be an abstract quality until a material vehicle was found for it. Time–space also finds its purpose as a property of animate matter: to govern the surrounding equilibrated environment by means of dissymmetry–irreversibility. Vernadskii does not reveal the mechanism of this governance, but he shows its result: it is analogous in its action to vast pressures and high temperatures. Some substances are formed within the earth but also in the biosphere under the influence of animate matter under normal conditions.[19]

All the other forms of time, which we call astronomical, geological, physical, and historical, are formed against the background of biological time, just as all space is formed against the background of dissymmetrical space. "Perhaps billions of years correspond to terrestrial planetary time and comprise only a small part of biological time," Vernadskii proposes.[20]

Thus Vernadskii found the real source of irreversibility–dissymmetry or the cause of the state of space–time.

Let us now recall what sort of time was superseded during his "Crimean vision." Was it the time that ordinary common sense and science usually identify with the universal movement of material and energy in the world, that is, the time of physical formulas? Of course not. What was superseded was real biological time, by which every person lives under the conditions of his own vital activity. Consciousness lives outside instinct. Reason exists outside space and time. Every thinking person intuitively senses this "speed" and essence.

But no one except Vernadskii gave Reason the cosmic natural sense that indeed is associated with the timelessness and spacelessness of its own activity. An actively functioning brain surmounts the "coerciveness" of biological time.[21]

It seems to me that, having revealed the reality of space–time, Vernadskii presented the most weighty proof of the unity of the cosmos, in which life is the only force capable of imparting irreversibility to all observable processes. At the same time, in my view, he gave a profound grounding to his initially intuitive concept of the "eternity of life." If we now switch from a scientific language to a philosophical language, we can try more accurately to define this time-like property.

Eternity as a continuous and unending succession of years is so-called bad infinity. In other words, it is an open-ended eternity, an eternity unfolding in time, produced by the animate matter of an eternally young biosphere. The dissymmetrical character of the living material causes the eternal "decline," the "duration" of time. Vernadskii extends this term of Bergson's to apply to the whole of life and not only to internal-intuitive activity.

Another eternity that became manifest in pointing out the source of dissymmetry–irreversibility is good infinity, closed in on itself. This is another order, another level of being—life without time and space, in other words, spiritual life. The world of ideas, information, or the sphere of action of the individual person acquires its own independent being, also based on time-like properties. It is in this capacity that Vernadskii calls reason a "cosmic force."[22]

Both types of eternity are of equal value, are real, and occasion the paradoxes of life's "appearing" in geological time and of rational life's appearing in biological time. Actually, they do not appear, since they are sufficient unto themselves, but "become manifest" only when these two velocities, these two regimes of time are compared.

An isolated island of thought

Vernadskii tried to bring his new views to his colleagues. In 1929 he prepared the collection *Animate Matter* [Zhivoe veshchestvo], which was to have opened with his lecture "The Beginning and the Eternity of Time" [Nachalo i vechnost' zhizni]. But a purge descended on the Academy, accompanied by the destruction of publishing houses, revisions of plans, and the arrest of directors. The collection was returned to its author and was preserved in a single bound copy.

History exactly repeated itself in 1936. It was only in 1940 that Vernadskii released the book, but now under a title that was not so provocative— *Biogeochemical Essays* [Biogeokhimicheskie ocherki]—and without the introductory article. Vernadskii himself removed it, although he understood that in doing so he was diminishing the philosophical impact of the book but on the other hand helping it get through censorship. Even after the author's death, censorship forced the compilers to "edit" the article in the collected writings. It was first published without distortions in 1989.

At the same time, Vernadskii published several pamphlets, under the collective title *Problems of Biogeochemistry* [Problemy biogeokhimii], which were extremely important for understanding the idea of eternity and each of which was accompanied by an infamous notice by the Editorial and Publishing Council of the Academy acknowledging Academician Vernadskii's service to science but disagreeing with his idealistic philosophical views. However, the third number, which gave the clearest presentation of the epistemological problems, was lost in the publishing house, and Vernadskii had to reconstruct it during the war, during his evacuation in Kazakhstan. Conscious of the particular importance of the essay, which presented the new natural science in most complete form, Vernadskii asked the Academy to print it in English instead of the Festschrift being prepared for his eightieth birthday. But without success. The essay did not appear in print until 1980.[23]

Also not so long ago, and moreover with editorial corrections, cuts, and "unmasking" commentary, the scholar's two principal books, written after he had acquired his new world view, were printed. They were begun in 1936 (when he was 73 years old!) as a "book of life," the summation of a lifetime, but the work soon divided into two parts. One, *Scientific Thought as a Planetary Phenomenon* [Nauchnaia mysl' kak planetnoe iavlenie], was printed for the first time in 1975, and the other, *The Chemical Structure of the Earth's Biosphere and Its Surroundings* [Khimicheskoe stroenie biosfery Zemli i ee okruzhenie], first came out in 1965.

Vernadskii's isolation both in his homeland and abroad lasted for a quarter of a century; after 1936 he ceased (not by choice) traveling abroad. The scattered individual articles and books on the new problems that were printed before that year did not make an integral impression. What is more, one must not forget that those were the years of the triumphal procession of the theory of relativity, with its new ideas about physical time–space. World scientific opinion was hardly able to digest one more, even "crazier," theory of time such as Vernadskii's idea about biological time–space.

And what happened with the second part of the Crimean prophecy, about the Institute? Understanding the special conditions of our country, Vernadskii founded a modest Biogeochemical Laboratory in 1928. It, like all the others that did not bring prompt military advantage to the rulers, dragged out a sorry existence, receiving none of the materials it needed.

The war began. Vernadskii was evacuated to Borovoe and the laboratory to Kazan'. In 1943 it was renamed the Laboratory for Geochemical Problems (now without the "bio"), and in that form it became part of the large institute, which today bears Vernadskii's name, created in 1946 under the nuclear program.

But the laboratory that gave birth to the Institute gradually disappeared. Its fate clearly demonstrates the lack of understanding of Vernadskii's main idea. The laboratory did not get new people and simply died out. Physically.

Thus, despite the abundance of students in the geological disciplines, Vernadskii had no successors in biogeochemistry. Nor, strictly speaking, did such a scientific specialty ever exist. It was gradually transformed into ecology, a science very remote from Vernadskii's idea. Both the intellectual and living (teacher-to-student) bond and continuity were lost. The energy of thought was gone.

The reasons, of course, were not just the conditions of our unhappy times, nor even scholarly stupidity, nor, if you will, scholarly snobbism.

Science, like the post office, accepts only small and well-wrapped packages. The theory of eternity cannot be said to be thoroughly worked out—Vernadskii simply did not have time to do this. Let us not forget his age. In 1916, when he became a scientist of a different sort, he was already

53 years old. It was time to sum up, not begin something new. Vernadskii preserved clarity of mind and a tremendous capacity for work down to his last day. (He wrote many times in the 1930s in his diary about his young mind in an increasingly decrepit body, about his brain, being killed by an aging body—one more demonstration of life's two different speeds.) But the volume of the new knowledge revealed to him was so vast that Vernadskii did not have time to present it adequately. He counted more on our understanding than on the clarity of his language. His articles contain many minor mistakes and contradictions, which are inevitable in the flux of thought. He is difficult, hard to grasp. The essence of his idea is not presented, as in Einstein, in one single small article but is spread among all the books and articles of the 1930s and, moreover, throughout the whole of his creative legacy.

Vernadskii began one of his last talks to his colleagues in Borovoe with the following sentence: "My scientific life has developed in such a way that, from my youthful years down to the present, I have been working scientifically at the frontiers of the scientific understanding we have achieved of reality."[24] Of course, it is not easy to be at a frontier. It is as if one has ended up on an uninhabited island where nothing is named yet. The principal difficulty appears to be terminological.

Vernadskii did not have time to create his own terminological corpus, which would reflect the new and at the same time incorporate the generally accepted. Even the word 'eternity', for example, cannot serve as a scientific concept since it has a vast tradition of being used in other languages—the language of philosophy and religion. Sometimes Vernadskii even consciously tried not to invent a new term and preferred either to expand the content of an old term or to narrow its scope. That is what occurred with the concept "animate matter," which Buffon already used to mean the indestructible "atoms of life" that passed from organism to organism.[25] After Vernadskii, the concept was compromised by the Lysenkoists, who used it to refer to some extracellular plasma supposed to generate cells.

The *Great Soviet Encyclopedia* now defines animate matter as the totality of the planet's living organisms existing at a particular moment in the biosphere and fulfilling a specific biogeochemical functions in it. A correct but very inadequate definition. Without being reinforced by the categories of time and space, it loses all specificity and is reduced to living beings, biotas, and other concepts from the fields of biology and ecology, while in a spatio-temporal sense, animate matter is a general scientific concept relating to the whole of reality.

The concept of biological time did not take root, did not have time to take root. It developed in science independently of Vernadskii and signifies chronobiology or biorhythmology, which study the behavior of living systems over time, in other words, the way external influences are reflected in the internal processes of living things, for example, circadian or seasonal cycles. From Vernadskii's standpoint, external rhythms are not time at all (as we know, St. Augustine already said that time cannot be equated with movement; it flows not because the stars and the planets rotate), but the science of biological time in this sense exists with its models, theories, and concrete investigations.

Vernadskii's more rigorous and precise terms, such as, for example, duration, dissymmetry, irreversibility, are little discussed. And no one at all knows the term 'layers of reality', which belongs in this list and refers to layers of being—layers of the universe, to be more precise—that are qualitatively different from space–time.[26] But most importantly, all of Vernadskii's most important works of the last twenty-five years of his life are not perceived as a whole, as a reflection of a central idea.

Vernadskii could not avoid pondering this position of his in the history of knowledge, his place in the world, more precisely speaking. Like Goethe, who posed himself only one single question "What is Goethe?" and spent his whole life answering it, so, too, Vernadskii saw that man is a planetary phenomenon, an actor of nature, and that his rational state is his nature. He is linked to the Cosmos only through reason, insofar as he is not only the thinking and suffering nerve of the universe but also its operative organ. Thought is everything, he said, although we are not sure how it is propagated or how it operates. Thought—what kind of energy is it, indeed?

Sensing in it his union with the Whole, Vernadskii also did not experience any melancholy from his solitude. He related to it tranquilly, as something normal and not pathological. A person should be alone. In 1928 Vernadskii wrote to Natal'ia Egorovna (and she copied down the thought, which struck her):

> I remember a youthful conversation that I often have occasion to recall, and I sense a vital truth that I stated at that time in paradoxical form: on an uninhabited island, without any hope of disclosing to anyone one's ideas and achievements, scientific discoveries, or artistic creations, without any hope of escaping—should one alter the creative work of one's thought, or should one continue to live, create, and work as if one lived in society and were striving to leave a trace of one's work in as manifest and explicit a form as possible? I decided that one should work precisely that way—I thought and think that an idea and its expression are not lost even if no one finds out about the intellectual creativity that took place on this isolated island. . . . Now as an old man I think that it is impossible ever to know the insurmountability of a barrier—an isolated island in time . . .
>
> I look at the future very calmly, since I see an elemental planetary process

that as a natural process is independent of man's will and his activity. The mystery of life is not clear, but the intimate connection of life with the past, the creation of human reason and the development of the brain containing it, over whole generations of organisms, always in the same direction for at least two billion years—these thrusts cannot be diverted from their proper course by any events of human history.[27]

In a scientific respect, of course, solitude is not a negative, pessimistic idea. Truth is not comprehended in any but a personal way. What is collectively elaborated is only what a single person has achieved at the boundary of an understanding of reality. There is no "fuel" in a collective that would take one there—no innermost spiritual union with the world, not expressible in words, no sense of oneself as an island of eternity in the midst of flowing, enveloping time.

It is no accident that in his historical-scientific works Vernadskii always looked at the scientist as a whole—he meditated on the religiosity of Newton and Faraday and on the esthetic feeling, the sense of universal harmony, that moved Kepler.

However, solitude cannot remain solitude forever. One must come out and create a scientific language for communication in a normal regime of time. And what is a merit there, personal uniqueness, at times here becomes the flaw of unintelligibility.

But science already sees the archipelago where Vernadskii's island is situated. Not recognizing the nameplates he set out, the sciences invent new titles, usually very pretty and memorable ones. Thus arose the "Gaia system" or Anthropy principle. In its interpretation of the coordination among all of the fundamental world constants and life, it is very much in accord with Vernadskii's idea. Since life creates its own medium, why should it not also create all the physical constants of this medium?

All such theories chip off bits from the idea of the eternity of life. And it is here that it is evident that science is not what but how; it is concerned not with the content but with the correctness of its constructs, and magnitude has no importance. By resolving the small problems, science will reach even the frontier that Vernadskii frequented.

Such ideas as the eternity of life should of course be discussed in philosophy. Only philosophy in the free flight of thought is capable of looking directly into Vernadskii's eyes. It is idle, of course, to think that it should be capable of resolving even a single scientific problem. It is time to forget about "scientific philosophy"—that oxymoron of Soviet thought. On the other hand, it can create an intellectual atmosphere around a scientific problem. Such an intellectual environment has not yet been created around Vernadskii's theory, despite the abundant literature about him.

Notes

1. *Druzhba narodov*, 1991, no. 3.
2. V.S. Neopolitanskaia, "Akty spravedlivosti," *Nauka i zhizn'*, 1988, no. 3.
3. The creators of the unique Biosphere-II in the American state of Arizona trace their scientific pedigree to Vernadskii. See D. Allen and M. Nel'son, *Kosmicheskie biosfery* (Moscow: Progress, 1991).
4. V.I. Vernadskii, "Iz dnevnikov 1919–1920 gg.," *Nauka i zhizn'*, 1988, no. 3, pp. 46–54. Jean-Antoine Condorcet was secretary of the Paris Academy of Sciences and member of the Revolutionary Convention of 1793. He was forced to hide. For several months he lived clandestinely near Paris and wrote his work *Sketches of a Historical Picture of the Progress of Human Reason* [Eskiz istoricheskoi kartiny progressa chelovecheskogo razuma] (last Russian edition, St. Petersburg, 1909), in which, following Turgot, he substantiated the idea of progress.
5. *Prometei* (Moscow), 1988, no. 15, pp. 112–19.
6. "Dnevnik za 22 ianv. 1936 g.," Archive of the Russian Academy of Sciences [hereafter ARAN], f. 519, op. 2, d. 7, l. 44.
7. H. Bergson, *Dlitel'nost' i odnovremennost'* (Petrograd, 1922).
8. V.I. Vernadskii, " 'Ia ne mogu uiti v odnu nauku . . .'—Iz pisem k N.E. Vernadskoi," *Prometei* (Moscow), 1988, no. 15, p. 100.
9. Ibid., p. 117.
10. A description of nature should not be based on the Holy Scriptures, and religious revelation should not be reinforced by scientific arguments, says V.N. Il'in in two of his interesting books, in which he shows that a biblical text is not an answer but a question and that both science and religion are equally incapable of giving us a plan and a system for the universe. See V.N. Il'in, *Zagadka zhizni i proiskhozhdenie zhivykh sushchestv* (Paris, 1929); V.N. Il'in, *Shest' dnei tvoreniia* (Paris, 1930).
11. *Prometei*, p. 112.
12. "Dnevnik, 2 aprelia 1921 g.," ARAN, f. 518, op. 2, d. 11, l. 299.
13. V.I. Vernadskii, *Nachalo i vechnost' zhizni* (Moscow, 1989), p. 107.
14. Condorcet ended his days here. Abandoning his refuge, he attempted to go abroad, but in Bourg-la-Reine he was recognized, captured, and thrown into prison; not wanting to fall into the hands of the Jacobins, he committed suicide on the prison straw.
15. V.I. Vernadskii, "O sostoianiiakh fizicheskogo prostranstva," *Filosofskie mysli naturalista* (Moscow, 1988), p. 273.
16. In the 1920s and 1930s, Vernadskii spoke about dissymmetry in almost every one of his works. See V.I. Vernadskii, "O pravizne i levizne" and "O korennom material'no-energeticheskom otlichii kosnykh i zhivykh tel biosfery," in *Problemy biogeokhimii*, vol. 16 of *Trudy biogeokhimicheskoi laborotorii* (Moscow, 1980).
Generally speaking, dissymmetry is a gross disequilibrium. In the spatio-chemical or thermodynamic sense, every particle of something living is in a sense raised to a height from which under the effects of entropy it "falls" continuously and in its movement accomplishes all external work. This is the state with the least possible entropy at the given level of energy.
An analog of dissymmetry is Irvin Bauer's principle of stable disequilibrium: "Living systems, and only living systems, are never in equilibrium; by the expenditure of their free energy they continually work against the equilibrium demanded by the laws of physics and chemistry under existing external conditions" (Irvin Bauer, *Teoreticheskaia biologiia* [Moscow–Leningrad, 1939]). Bauer showed that all the energy of an organism is expended not on external work but to sustain disequilibrium,

and the work is accomplished spontaneously. Philosophy is silent about dissymmetry, but dissymmetry is applicable to everything, for example, architecture or psychology. Our fear of everything synthetic—clothes, medicines—is the instinctive protest of everything living against a racemic compound.

17. V.I. Vernadskii, "O sostoianiiakh prostranstva v geologicheskikh iavleniiakh. Na fone rosta nauki XX stoletiia," *Trudy*, p. 130.

18. V.I. Vernadskii, "O zhiznennom (biologicheskom) vremeni," *Filosofskie mysli naturalista*, pp. 297–381.

19. V.I. Vernadskii, "O biologicheskom znachenii nekotorykh biokhimicheskikh proiavleniiakh zhizni," *Priroda*, 1988, no. 2, pp. 33–38.

20. V.I. Vernadskii, "Izuchenie iavlenii zhizni i novaia fizika," *Trudy*, p. 275. Vernadskii assumes that biological time is equal in duration to geological time, that it is one and the same time. His hypothesis that we will not find in the earth's crust—that is, in other words, in the geological past—layers free of the influence of life has been brilliantly reinforced for almost half a century. At that time the age of the Earth was calculated as 1.5 billion years, and now it is calculated as 4.5 billion. And life stubbornly moves along with the radiogeology that determines age. Paleontologists find traces of life in strata 3.8 billion years old, and geochemistry discovers the biogenetic character of the carbon of the most ancient rocks. Thus the age of life is comparable to hypothetical cosmic periods of existence of the Universe, which adds a further enigma to the phenomenon of life.

21. The need to reduce the problem of space–time to irreversibility–dissymmetry was also stressed by P.A. Florenskii. In one of his last letters to his son (from Solovki), he wrote:

> The principal task of natural science is to demonstrate the reality of space–time, that is, its irreducibility to an abstract concept about order and the balance of something that is spaceless and timeless (as the rationalists did), or to an association (conditional reflex) of psychological elements (as representatives of sensualism of various stripes did). The opposite answer spells the end for natural science itself—if the reality of its object, nature, is taken away, it makes no sense to study what does not exist but only seems to exist, however forcefully (Kant). The most weighty proof of the reality of space–time is found in the fact that asymmetry [Florenskii means here dissymmetry—G.A.] and irreversibility exist in nature. Asymmetry, in the spatial aspect of the world, and irreversibility, in time. [Quoted from a copy kindly provided by P.V. Florenskii, to whom the author expresses deep thanks.]

Probably one should add to this statement that the localization of dissymmetry–irreversibility grounds both rationalism as a science of a timeless and spaceless object and its method—reason.

22. V.I. Vernadskii, "Avtotrofnost' chelovechestva," *Trudy*, p. 228.

23. Ibid., pp. 85–164.

24. V.I. Vernadskii, "O geologicheskikh obolochkakh zemli kak planety," *Sobranie sochinenii* (Moscow, 1959), vol. 4, p. 90.

25. G.P. Aksenov, "Poniatie zhivogo veshchestva: ot Biuffona do Vernadskogo," *Voprosy istorii estestvoznaniia i tekhniki*, 1988, no. 1, pp. 57–66.

26. G.P. Aksenov, "Mir po Vernadskomu," *Priroda*, 1992, no. 5.

27. "Khronologiia V.I. Vernadskogo," ARAN, f. 518, op. 2, d. 28, l. 46.

N.K. GAVRIUSHIN

The Cosmic Route to "Eternal Bliss"

(K.E. Tsiolkovskii and the Mythology
of Technocracy)

I remember a conversation that took place twenty years ago in one of the rooms of the Institute of the History of the Natural Sciences and Technology of the USSR Academy of Sciences.

"Please don't get angry with me," repeated the elderly professor in a major-general's uniform to his scientific and technical colleague who had graduated from the Philosophy Faculty two years before, "but this is a 'quirk' you have ... Of course I know that having a 'quirk' means you're Russian ... But, you see, I have spent half my life putting Tsiolkovskii on a pedestal, and here you are digging up his weakest works."

"But what about the ideals of science, Arkadii Aleksandrovich," said the young seeker of truth, not yielding his ground. "What about historical authenticity?"

"Let me tell you something," answered the general after a minute of silence. "When I was preparing the *Collected Works* of Konstantin Eduardovich for publication, I found a mistake in his derivation of the formula for rocket movement. The result was correct, but there was a mistake in the calculations ... but I couldn't present Tsiolkovskii in that way! I of course recalculated everything, and now everything there is perfectly in order."

Thus the sides had defined their positions definitively. But there is no need to hurry with a moral assessment of them. The dispute between A.A. Kozmodem'ianskii, deeply devoted to the ideals of science, and the author of these lines was of course not only about the possibility of publishing a

Russian text © 1992 by "Nauka" Publishers and "Voprosy filosofii." "Kosmicheskii put' k 'vechnomu blazhenstvu' (K.E. Tsiolkovskii i mifologiia tekhnokratii)," *Voprosy filosofii*, 1992, no. 6, pp. 125–31. A publication of the Institute of Philosophy, Russian Academy of Sciences.

Nikolai Konstantinovich Gavriushin is a senior scientific associate of the Institute of the History of Natural Science and Technology of the Russian Academy of Sciences.

report on Tsiolkovskii's atomistics. Kozmodem'ianskii was very concerned with preserving the "religion of technocracy," regardless of how clearly he was aware of this, and was protecting one of its revered "icons," while his young opponent, who since his student days had set himself to refute this religion, was concealing his destructive designs under the banner of being scientific . . .

That conflict was resolved quite well: the article was printed in a mimeo-graphed collection, and the pedestal of the founder of theoretical cosmonautics suffered not in the least. But the myth of K.E. Tsiolkovskii's "cosmic philosophy" is an integral part of technocratic pseudoreligiosity to this day and hence calls for a dispassionate analysis.

* * *

That Konstantin Eduardovich Tsiolkovskii (1857–1935) was a religious thinker with distinct features of prophetic consciousness—of this there can be no doubt. One of his first scientific works, "Calculations and Formulas on the Question of Interplanetary Communications" [Vychisleniia i formuly otnosiashchiesia k voprosu o mezhplanetnykh soobshcheniiakh] (1879) has the very significant subheading "The Question of Eternal Bliss" [Vopros o vechnom blazhenstve]. The question is as old as the world itself, and the belief that it can be resolved technically and instrumentally is also by no means a novelty. The only problem is in inventing these instruments—in this case, dirigibles and a space rocket.

No less important was believing in the authentic reality of "eternal bliss" or the "Kingdom of God." Two "heavenly signs," which Tsiolkovskii received in 1884 in the city of Borovsk, played a role in this: one of these was the appearance of a cloud in the form of the Cross, and the other was a cloud in the form of a human face.[1] Doubts were dispelled, and he was able to say quite resolutely: "Christ's teaching arouses a very profound reverence and faith in many people. And I am one of these people."[2]

It remained for him only to determine his relation to the Church, as the repository of this teaching, and his attitude toward science, which outwardly contradicted the religious world view. Tsiolkovskii resolved the first question for himself quite uncompromisingly. "Rituals," he wrote, "are useless vestiges of previously rational actions," there are no mysteries, and as for the clergy, "what is the sense of this institution when until recently the chief procurator commanded them like soldiers?"[3]

Tsiolkovskii, who deeply believed in his exceptional gifts and purpose from youth ("I am such a great man as has never been before, nor will ever be"),[4] took it upon himself to explain questions of faith from the very beginning, without burdening himself at all with ecclesiastical Tradition. In 1887 he created his own variant of the Lord's Prayer,[5] and in 1898 he reworked it into a small composition, "An Explanation of the Lord's Prayer and Its Expression in Living Words" [Raz''iasnenie molitvy gospodnei i vyrazhenie ee zhivymi slovami].[6]

Then Tsiolkovskii wrote "The Scientific Foundations of Religion" [Nauchnye osnovaniia religii], in which his world-view positions are set out quite definitively and for a long time to come. He expresses the hope that science and faith will some day become one,[7] and he sets out his theory of atomistic panpsychism, which he reproduced almost unchanged in "The Monism of the Universe" [Monizm Vselennoi] (1925, 1931) and a number of other works.

The concept of "scientific faith" appears for the first time in Tsiol-kovskii's "Scientific Foundations of Religion." He opposes this concept to the "unruliness of the imagination" of everyday faith. "Scientific faith" presupposes a critical attitude toward the facts and hypotheses of contemporary science. "Science exists for an instant," he wrote later, "and is advancing every minute. Can one say what it will give us in thousands or in millions of years? If a century is sufficient to turn everything upside down in it and in man's view of the world, then what will things be like in a thousand millennia?"[8]

Later on Tsiolkovskii would turn many times to an analysis of the events of evangelical history from the positions of this "scientific faith," persistently seeking possible "natural" explanations of supernatural events, miracles, and healings. In this respect, his reasoning about Christ's resurrection is very characteristic.

"Why not assume the limitedness of our knowledge," writes Tsiol-kovskii, "and admit that unknown forces of heaven and its higher beings inaccessible to our senses played a part here? Of course this is only a bewitching dream, but we at least admit its possibility. We do not forget that our science has existed only for an instant, that in this instant it has altered its direction many times, and it has more than once burned what it had worshipped."[9]

However, quite often Tsiolkovskii reduces his "natural" explanations of miracles to simple visual aberrations and illusionism, and from his point of view Lazarus's resurrection turns out to be a consciously organized spectacle in which even Jesus himself was led astray. "We do not take the resurrection of Lazarus as a conscious deception on the part of Jesus, as a conspiracy with Lazarus. Jesus was too great a person for that. But his friend Lazarus and his family were worldly people. Without fully under-standing their teacher, they were extremely well-disposed toward him and tried with all their might to help him catch the attention of the crowd, overturn the domination of the pagans (Romans), and establish the kingdom of truth. That is what could have served as a deception for Jesus and the people around him."[10]

Finally, there is one other motif in Tsiolkovskii's explanation of the events of Sacred history in the Old and New Testaments. He was prepared to regard many of them as expressions of the "dreams" of humanity about the future achievements of science and technology. "Jesus's miracles, which can be explained naturally," he wrote, "nonetheless are remarkable as dreams that mankind is more and more realizing right now. . . . The productivity of labor has increased tenfold, a hundredfold, and a thousandfold. Does not this justify over time Jesus's words about birds that do not plow, do not harvest, but are always sated? The victories of science and technology are more striking than great miracles."[11] Tsiolkovskii was inclined to regard even the virginity of the Mother of God as a dream "about the future woman, who will provide children but will not be subject to animal passions": parthenogenesis is a means for "continually improving the human race."[12]

The above is quite sufficient to put together a general idea of the character of the "theological" reasoning of K.E. Tsiolkovskii. (We should just point out that a textual comparison of his writings with the religious works of Lev Tolstoi sometimes yields interesting results.)[13] It is important for us to see that Tsiolkovskii's "cosmic philosophy" is a religious philosophy and that an essential component of it is the aspiration to achieve as full as possible a correspondence between the images and concepts of Christianity and the most recent scientific ideas in the domain of cosmology, biology, and so forth.

Tsiolkovskii was by no means alone in this aspiration toward a "scientific substantiation of religion." It was quite clearly delineated in the positivists—for example, Auguste Comte and Joseph Renan. John Fiske (1842–1901), the founder of the American version of "cosmic philosophy," basing himself mainly on the ideas of Herbert Spencer, thought that he had succeeded in fully eliminating the seeming antagonism between science and religion.[14]

But esoteric writings, in particular the most recent theosophy, which claimed to be a "synthesis" of science and religion, had a much greater influence on Tsiolkovskii than positivism, probably through his Kaluga surroundings.

Although Tsiolkovskii's library has not come down to us in its entirety, there are quite sufficient proofs that he was familiar with such literature. He himself expressed himself openly and clearly on this account: "In my view, the teaching of the occultists about man's being made up of many essences—astral, mental, and so forth—is antiscientific. I am far removed from these things, which are the result of a limited knowledge or the young enthusiasm of youthful impressions, which we cannot get out of our minds however we try, just as we cannot deny other impressions we received in childhood."[15]

This statement is highly revealing. Tsiolkovskii was never an adept of freemasonry, occultism, theosophy, and so on, both because of the relative speculative complexity of the components of their conceptions (the thicket of abstract arguments did not appeal to him) and because of his aspiration to build his own quite simple and all-embracing doctrine, justifying and explaining the direction of his engineering-inventive activity. But he shows the influence of occult teachings on his view of the world—an indelible influence—from his very young years. To establish accurately the range of Tsiolkovskii's reading would of course be very desirable but it is not essential, given the conservative nature of the esoteric doctrines: for example, the arguments about "invisible beings" in the book by G.F. Rettsel[16] (1784) differ very little from the corresponding passages in the book by Ledbiter[17] (1909) and from the analogous statements by Tsiolkovskii about "beings higher than man."[18]

Tsiolkovskii's cast of mind was consonant with a whole set of ideas of esoteric philosophy. This concerns above all the most important concepts and conceptual schemata of cosmism, such as "cosmic thinking," "cosmic consciousness," "the cosmic point of view," "cosmic citizenship," and so forth.

As regards "cosmic thinking," we shall limit ourselves to two quotations from Madame Blavatsky's works. "In modern language," she writes, "Divine thought would better be called cosmic thinking, or Spirit, and Akasha cosmic substance, or Matter,"[19] obviously choosing new names in keeping with the spirit of positive natural science in place of the Gnostic terms. "Our consciousness," she says in another place, "comes from Spirit, or Cosmic Thinking, and the various conductors in which this consciousness is individualized and achieves a reflective consciousness or self-consciousness come from cosmic substance."[20]

The book by R.M. Bucke entitled *Cosmic Consciousness*, which originated in the same circles and was translated into almost all the principal European languages, helped to spread this concept of "cosmic consciousness."

The concept of universal citizenship, which expresses an orientation toward a cosmological substantiation of ethics that is especially characteristic of esoteric doctrines (and stoicism), is used persistently, for example, by Karl du Prel: "If a person is a citizen of the Universe, ethics is possible; but if he is only a citizen of the earth, then no ethical task exists; there exists only a social task"; "the task of philosophy and religion is to cultivate in man a consciousness of his universal citizenship."[21] In du Prel we find already the call, characteristic later of Tsiolkovskii as well, to adopt a "cosmic viewpoint."[22]

Central to this system of Tsiolkovskii's views was, as we know, the idea of the "sensate atom," which has counterparts both in the history of materialist doctrines (Lucretius, Haeckel, Morozov, etc.)[23] and in esoterism. Here are a few quotations from a popular book by Annie Besant, who in turn based herself on the "pioneering" work of Blavatsky's entitled *The Secret Doctrine.*

"The selfsame infinitely small *invisible lives* constitute the atoms of a mountain and a chamomile, a man and an ant, an elephant and the tree protecting it from the sun. Every particle—you may call it organic or inorganic—*is life*. Every atom and molecule in the Universe is at the same time *giving life* and *giving death* to this form."[24] The idea, so important for Tsiolkovskii, that an atom "sleeps" in inorganic matter is quite clearly discernible here: "Occultism does not recognize anything inorganic in the cosmos. The term 'inorganic substance' used in science signifies simply that the latent life slumbering in the molecules of so-called 'inert matter' is unknowable." Hence the idea quite naturally arises of an all-pervasive hierarchy of forms of consciousness: "Everything in the Universe, in all its kingdoms, is consciousness, that is, is endowed with a consciousness of its species and its own plane of perception."[25]

The logical development of this conception is the idea of the sensibility of *space* as some primal reality and the potentiality of all that exists. The following statement by Madame Blavatsky is characteristic in this connection: "Space, regarded as the unity of substance—the living Source of Life—in the capacity of the 'Unknowable Uncaused Cause' is the most ancient dogma in occultism, incomparably more ancient than the Ether (Pater-Aether) of the ancient Greeks and Latins. Likewise, Force and Matter, as potentialities of Space, are inseparable and express the Unknowable."[26]

The idea of space as the "sensor of God" is characteristic, in particular, of Isaac Newton as well, with whom Tsiolkovskii had many points of contiguity, including points relating to this particular question.[27]

It is quite probable that the idea, linked to the same tradition, of a periodic consolidation of matter and of the rational beings formed by it (as well as the coexistence of beings of different cosmic epochs) had an influence on Tsiolkovskii's cosmogonic theory. This conception, which is also close to stoicism, is found in Madame Blavatsky, Rudolf Steiner, and others.

Finally, there are at least two more aspects in which one may assume an influence of theosophic literature on Tsiolkovskii. One of these concerns the question of the social role of geniuses (there is every reason for supposing that he was familiar with Edouard Schuré's book *Great Initiates* [Velikie posviashchennye]), and the other, a specifically theological set of issues (the "cause of the cosmos").

Another circumstance worthy of special attention is that the two theoretical systems that had the most influence on Tsiolkovskii—Darwinian–Spencerian evolutionism and theosophical esoterism—have much in common. Thus Blavatsky readily noted points of view in common between theosophy and Spencer's philosophy. She wrote:

> Herbert Spencer has recently toned down his agnosticism so much that he has found it possible to maintain that the nature of the "First Cause," which an occultist would much more logically derive from the Uncaused Cause, and the nature of the "Eternal" and the "Unknowable" are essentially homogeneous with the consciousness that streams over us—in other words, that the impersonal reality pervading the whole cosmos is a pure noumenon of thought. This progress in his thought brings him very close to an esoteric interpretation and to the teaching of the Vedanta.[28]

Karl du Prel expressed himself even more definitely: "From a cosmic point of view," he wrote, "one can say that there exists an infinite multitude of worlds, an infinite multitude of species of both corporeal and spiritual adaptation, an infinite multitude of subjective worlds, that is, representations of the world, an infinite multitude of kinds of experience and response. Thus, mysticism is, in a sense, a continuation of Darwinism."[29]

A comparison of the positions of Tsiolkovskii with the ideas of du Prel is in general rather interesting. In his article "The Struggle for Existence in Celestial Space (An Application of Darwin's Formula to Heavenly Mechanics)" [Bor'ba za sushchestvovanie v nebesnom prostranstve (prilozhenie formuly Darvina k nebesnoi mekhanike)], du Prel, first, states what is perhaps the most important idea in the system of Tsiolkovskii's views—the idea that it is necessary to recognize the "capacity for sensation as the basic property of all of matter." "The continuing dispute between materialism and spiritualism," he continues, "will conclude, in all likelihood, with our acknowledging that the sensation of organized matter is only an elevation of the basic property inherent in all matter."[30]

Here, too, du Prel puts forth the idea, no less important for Tsiolkovskii, that in the cosmos perfection reigns and an almost complete liberation from suffering is achieved: "We will reach an understanding of the phenomena of cosmic harmony only when we recognize the constellations and movements of the members of the stellar organism as states in which the sum of possible unpleasant sensations is reduced to its minimum."[31]

Thus, in du Prel we find panpsychic ideas, a cosmic grounding of ethics, the ideal of liberation from suffering realized in the movement of the heavenly bodies. But even that is not all; he also makes a very transparent allusion to the possibility of the *physical* subjugation of cosmic space. He writes:

> One can imagine that relations will one day be established between our planet, which appears today as an island isolated in the ocean of world space, and the rest of the world. There is no need to understand this comparison literally and dream about future journeys to the moon or to Mars, although one can hope that things will be the same for us as for primitive man, who once stood on the seashore as helpless as we today stand before the atmospheric ocean, until one time, with a heart of stone in his breast, as Horace puts it, he dared to venture onto the waves in his frail boat.[32]

There is no room for doubt about the deep connection between theosophic mysticism and cosmism, just as there can be no doubt about their connection with Darwinian–Spencerian evolutionism and positivist natural philosophy in general.

The connection between cosmism and the traditions of social utopianism is also quite clear. Thus Charles Fourier was convinced that the theory of social, animal, organic, and material movements he discovered was valid not only for the Earth but also for other planets, and that only this theory makes it possible for societies of rational beings to achieve prosperity. Moreover, this scientific theory claims to ground and explain the truths of Christian dogma. Fourier maintains that mankind is destined to remain on earth for 80,000 years, after which people's souls will once again rejoin matter in other worlds, on whose well-being will depend the realization of the hope for "eternal bliss."

Fourier divides this interval of time into four phases (two of them 5 years each and two 35,000 years) and thirty-two periods, accompanied by certain natural phenomena. In particular, he predicts a gradual shift in the orientation of the earth's axis, which will culminate with its fixation on the Sun and will bring the earth to a natural death. However, before this comes about, mankind, which will have passed from "civilization" to a "societary system," will have extended its economic activity far beyond the sixtieth northern parallel, and the climate of the planet will have become much milder and more regular, accompanied by the ever more frequent appearance of the northern lights, which ultimately will assume the stable form of a broad band or corona in the vicinity of the pole. This corona will symbolize

progress on Earth and at the same time will contribute to the further improvement of natural conditions.

Thus, at the very beginning of the nineteenth century, Fourier predicted
that the activity of mankind should in the near future assume a general
planetary character and that the "northern corona," symbolizing this qualitatively new stage [of mankind's activity], would be a natural expression of
the progress of the "noosphere," to use a term of Vernadskii's, Le Roi's,
and Teilhard de Chardin's.

It is at this point, according to Fourier, that mankind will become part of
the community of cosmic civilizations, which are at a higher level of
development. According to his belief, the inhabitants of heavenly bodies
having a ring, like Saturn, escape savagery, barbarism, and civilization and
throughout all of their development retain a higher, "serial" system of social
life.

How strongly Fourier tied his natural philosophy to Christian revelation,
long before Fiske and Tsiolkovskii, may be inferred from his reflections on
the galaxy as a huge self-regulating system. Fourier thought that the birth of
the Godman–Christ on earth coincided with the beginning of the decline of
solar activity and that substantial changes supposedly took place in the
starry heavens simultaneously with supernatural help for mankind . . .

Fourier united his social utopia in the most direct manner with a program
of mankind's cosmic expansion, and Tsiolkovskii in this respect was merely
following a paradigm that had already been established. In his declining
years, he considered it to be to his credit that as early as "under the tsar he
had published a purely communist article ('Grief and Genius' [Gore i
genii])."[33] There was not the least exaggeration in these words. Tsiolkovskii
somewhat anticipated the Bolsheviks with his ideas of "war communism,"
although the radicalism he manifested proved in some respects unaccept-
able even to Lenin and Trotskii.

Simultaneously with his projects of social change, Tsiolkovskii developed a
purely technocratic scenario for improving social prosperity. Thus, in 1915
he argued that the economic effect of introducing his dirigible with an
all-metal shell would result in "capitalists' being satisfied with less and less
profit, until an ordinary 3–10 percent net income is achieved,"[34] and three
years later he presented an even more enticing picture: "Those without land
will comfortably resettle onto splendid free lands. . . . The activity of the
whole world will grow to the point that there will be no unemployed, and
wages will not rise fictitiously but will bring workers a truly glorious
existence."[35]

It is not so important who believed in these promises and projects at that
time. What is important is that those who are disposed to accept the "cosmic

philosophy" should be aware of the circumstances surrounding its origins, its internal contradictions, and the social and ecological consequences of the projects built on its basis. There is absolutely no way to eliminate from this philosophy the "theory of rational egoism," which, according to Tsiolkovskii, requires the destruction of "imperfect" forms of animal and plant life—no more and no less than all mammals and all of tropical nature. "Kill him who is suffering"—that was the most succinct formula of the cosmic path to "eternal bliss" of the omnipresent indestructible sensate atom, of the "citizen of the universe" without kin or memory. Setting about to govern mankind, this child of the idle fantasy of a scientific mind would actually carry out on Earth the "ideal order of social life" and, selecting the one best pair of people for propagation, would painlessly put away or castrate all the others . . .

* * *

In the early 1970s, with the recollection of which these reflections began, articles about the "cosmic" origin of religion would appear from time to time in the mass-circulation factory newspaper *Progress*, published in Kaliningrad outside Moscow. Those who had mastered the production of space rockets were using, one could say, their work tool to interpret the Sacred history of the Old and New Testaments. In the final analysis it was not so important for them whether mankind would one day be saved in spaceships or whether extraterrestrials would arrive in similar apparatuses to save it. As Heraclitus once said, "the way up and the way down are one and the same." In any case, they began to enlist the biblical patriarchs and apostles in the new mythology of technocracy.

This mythology is now going through the same crisis as the military-industrial complex, to which it largely owes its origins. Suddenly it has been replaced by the old mythology of a plutocracy, the cult of the "golden calf." But one can assume that this animal, free of suffering, will be able to put this "cosmic philosophy" to use in its own interests.

Notes

1. K.E. Tsiolkovskii, "Zapisi o sostoianii zdorov′ia (i dr.)," Archive of the Russian Academy of Sciences (hereinafter ARAN), f. 555, op. 2, ed. khr. 41, l. 5–5 verte.

2. K.E. Tsiolkovskii, "Nauchnye osnovaniia religii," ARAN, f. 555, op. 1, ed. khr. 370, l. 2.

3. K.E. Tsiolkovskii, "Galileiskii plotnik," ARAN, f. 555, op. 1, ed. khr. 438, l. 28.

4. K.E. Tsiolkovskii, *Grezy o Zemle i nebe* (Tula, 1986), p. 402.

5. K.E. Tsiolkovskii, ["Molitva"], ARAN, f. 55, op. 1, ed. khr. 369.

6. ARAN, f. 555, op. 1, ed. khr. 371.

7. "I have thought long and tirelessly about questions of faith in connection with scientific facts," writes Tsiolkovskii, "and I found in my reason much that confirms the foundations of faith. Much in it remained unclear to me, and many questions are not resolved at all. But since rational faith has great power and turns out to be quite close to the teachings of Christ, I do not think that its exposition would be harmful for society. Let there be two faiths: one the pure Christian teaching without any casuistry and intellectualizing, and the other scientific, limited, and incomplete. Perhaps a time will come when the two will come together in one" (ARAN, f. 555, op. 1, ed. khr. 370, l. 3 verte–4). Tsiolkovskii believed that in its essential world-view foundation this fusion had already come about. "According to Tsiolkovskii's *monism*, there is nothing besides perfect life. Jesus would understand this" ("Galileiskii plotnik," ARAN, f. 555, op. 1, ed. khr. 438, l. 9).

8. K.E. Tsiolkovskii, "Pervoprichina," ARAN, f. 55, op. 1, ed. khr. 393, l. 72.

9. K.E. Tsiolkovskii, "Voskresenie galileiskogo plotnika," ARAN, f. 555, op. 1, ed. khr. 406, l. 12.

10. K.E. Tsiolkovskii, "Predanie o zhizni i uchenii Khrista po Luke," ARAN, f. 555, op. 1, ed. khr. 405, l. 55.

11. Ibid., l. 56.

12. Tsiolkovskii, "Galileiskii plotnik," ARAN, f. 555, op. 1, ed. khr. 438, l. 5–6.

13. See N.K. Gavriushin, " 'K.E. Tsiolkovskii i L.N. Tolstoi (Doklad na X Chteniiakh K.E. Tsiolkovskogo, 1975 g.)," Archive of the K.E. Tsiolkovskii GMIK (Kaluga).

14. See J. Fiske, *Outlines of Cosmic Philosophy Based on the Doctrine of Evolution with Criticism on the Positive Philosophy* (Boston and New York, 1900), vols. 1–2. See also N.K. Gavriushin, " 'Kosmicheskaia filosofiia' Dzhona Fiska," *Trudy X i XI Chtenii K.E. Tsiolkovskogo. Sektsiia "K.E. Tsiolkovskii i filosofskie problemy osvoeniia kosmosa"* (Moscow: Institute of Philosophy, 1978), pp. 117–23.

15. K.E. Tsiolkovskii, "Zhivotnoe kosmosa," *Sobranie sochinenii* (Moscow, 1964), vol. 4, p. 303.

16. [G.F. Rettsel'], *Kratkoe izveshchenie o nevidimom sushchestve i o nakhodiashchikhsia v neizmerimom ego prostranstve tvariakh dobrykh i zlykh, takzhe zvezdnykh i stikhiinykh dukhakh, o proiskhozhdenii dukhov, sushchestve i deistvii ikh . . .* [Moscow, 1784].

17. Ch. Ledbiter, *Nevidimye pomoshchniki i nevidimyi mir* (Kaluga, 1909).

18. K.E. Tsiolkovskii, "Sushchestva vyshe cheloveka," ARAN, f. 555, op. 1, ed. khr. 499.

19. E.P. Blavatskaia, *Tainaia doktrina* (Berlin, 1915), p. 31.

20. E.P. Blavatskaia, " 'Prolog' k 'Tainoi doktrine,' " *Voprosy teosofii* (St. Petersburg), 1910, no. 2, p. 138.

21. K. Diu Prel', *Filosofiia mistiki, ili dvoistvennost' chelovecheskogo sushchestva*, trans. from the German by M.S. Aksenov (St. Petersburg, 1895), p. 558.

22. Ibid., p. xii. Cf., K.E. Tsiolkovskii's article "Neobkhodimost' kosmicheskoi tochki zreniia," *Istoriko-astronomicheskie issledovaniia* (Moscow), 1980, no. 15, p. 300.

23. See N.K. Gavriushin, "Tsiolkovskii i atomistika," *Trudy VII Chtenii K.E. Tsiolkovskogo. Sektsiia "Issledovanie nauchnogo tvorchestva K.E. Tsiolkovskogo"* (Moscow, 1973), pp. 36–50.

24. A. Besant, *The Seven Principles of Man* (London, 1892), pp. 8–9.

25. Ibid., pp. 63–64.

26. Blavatskaia, "Prolog," p. 131.

27. N.K. Gavriushin, "N'iuton i Tsiolkovskii (k tipologii tvorcheskikh ustanovok)," *Trudy XX Chtenii K.E. Tsiolkovskogo* (Moscow: IIET, 1987), pp. 3–11.

28. Blavatskaia, "Prolog," p. 134.

29. Diu Prel', *Filosofiia mistiki*, p. xii.

30. K. Diu Prel', "Bor'ba za sushchestvovanie v nebesnom prostranstve," *Znanie*, 1875, p. 102.

31. Ibid., p. 103.

32. Diu Prel', *Filosofiia mistiki*, p. 569. Cf., also, the "astral romances," for example, Th. Flournoy, *Des Indes à planète Mars* (Paris, 1900).

33. K.E. Tsiolkovskii, *Atlas dirizhablia iz volnistoi stali* (Kaluga, 1931), p. 22. The article "Gore i genii" was published as a separate brochure in Kaluga in 1916.

34. K.E. Tsiolkovskii, *Tablitsa dirizhablei iz volnistogo metalla* (Kaluga, 1915), p. 21.

35. K.E. Tsiolkovskii, *Vozhdushnyi transport* (Kaluga, 1918), p. 13.

V.P. FILATOV

The Living Cosmos

Man Among the Forces of Earth and Heaven

From the editors. Our society, too, is apparently not uninterested in problems associated with such mysterious phenomena of the human psyche as clairvoyance, telepathy, and telekinesis. Expectations and hopes with regard to psychosurgical intervention on the human organism thrive; ideas of reincarnation and life after death, the interaction of our civilization with supposed inhabitants and civilizations of the Universe (witness the fascination with the search for UFOs), the influence of the natural-cosmic environment on human destiny (astrology), or, on the contrary, man's independence of natural laws (levitation) are widespread. The corpus of these ideas has a life of its own (although one can hardly accuse the mass media of neglecting them), is becoming institutionalized, is successful in lobbying for its interests, and is becoming an influential force in society, generating a unique emotional atmosphere that combines fear of the future with hopes that fate is more favorable to man than would be warranted from the picture of the world painted by modern science.

The question arises: With what is this phenomenon associated; what are the real natural, social, and spiritual preconditions generating it as a cultural-historical phenomenon; what are the means, the factors, and the mechanisms of its transmission? The authors of the articles being published here attempt to answer this question. The very fact of posing this task dictates different types of responses, depending on the investigators' own value orientations, beliefs, and assimilated cultural traditions. But one thing is clear: it is time to take a calm, balanced, and close look at this set of problems through the eyes of theoretical-philosophical consciousness.

Russian text © 1994 by the Presidium of the Russian Academy of Sciences. "Zhivoi kosmos: chelovek mezhdu silami zemli i neba," *Voprosy filosofii*, 1994, no. 2, pp. 3–12. A publication of the Institute of Philosophy, Russian Academy of Sciences.

Vladimir Petrovich Filatov is a Doctor of Philosophical Sciences and department chair of the Russian State University for the Humanities (RGGU).

The purpose of the present article is to discuss the ever more frequent questions about the "cosmic" dimensions of human experience.[1] Discussions of mystical cosmic energies or of powerful forces of the Universe influencing man can be heard among the most varied circles: among believers in extra-sensory phenomena, among supporters of folk and nontraditional medicine, and among persons who adhere to various mystical, occult teachings.

Most often conversations about the cosmos and its influence on man remain obscure and are only a kind of sign of people's involvement with unusual, alternative types of knowledge and spiritual practices. Can some light be shed on these references to mysterious cosmic forces and influences? There are apparently various ways and means of doing this. Philosophy, too, is able to say something on the matter, insofar as it is capable of directing our attention to that perennial intellectual context that lies behind the cosmic perception of the world.

The harmony of the Cosmos

Let us begin with well-known matters. The history of ancient science and culture shows that "the cosmic perception of the world" was a universal and general human phenomenon, widespread over thousands of years in all the highly developed civilizations of antiquity: Egypt, Babylon, China, India, and ancient Greece. Until the West European scientific revolution of the sixteenth and seventeenth centuries, it provided the framework within which people's knowledge about nature, society, and man was accumulated and systematized. It is precisely this quality of fitting into an all-embracing and unique construction of the Cosmos that distinguishes the conceptions of our distant ancestors from contemporary forms of scientific knowledge, which are united by another, "noncosmic" paradigm of thinking.

What was this mysterious Cosmos, how can we understand and feel the overall spirit of such a perception of the world? The easiest way is by turning to ancient Greek notions of the Cosmos, since the thinkers of antiquity not only created the most harmonious and elaborate doctrines about it but also were simply enamored of the mysterious harmony of the cosmic spheres.

The word 'cosmos' itself, in its prescientific and prephilosophical sense, meant "order." It was used to designate a military unit in formation, a state structure, and even the attire of a woman who had put herself in "order" (hence the term 'cosmetics'). As for the "structure of the world," this term was first used by Heraclitus; Pythagoras taught about the musical and mathematical harmony of the Cosmos as a consequence of its rational and beautiful orderliness. Penetrating into and partaking of this harmony were regarded in the Pythagorean school (which was both a scientific and a mystical, religious-moral society) as ways of cleansing the human soul for the purpose of its salvation in the cycle of births and deaths.

The idea of the Cosmos was one of the key ideas of the culture of antiquity. If one looks more deeply into the variety of views of the ancient Greek thinkers, one will notice that the dominant feature of all of them was an understanding of the world as a finite, beautiful, and ordered whole circumscribed by set boundaries. All elements of existence are arranged in the hierarchical structures of the Cosmos and are bound together into a kind of single organism suffused by life. In Plato's dialogue *Timaeus*, that pinnacle of ancient cosmological thought, the great philosopher regards the Cosmos as the "only living being" and, after sketching a picture of the genesis and organization of the universe, concludes: "After taking into itself mortal and immortal animate beings and filling itself with them, our cosmos became a visible animate being uniting everything visible, a sensuous god, the image of a god attainable by reason, the greatest and the best, the most beautiful and the most perfect, the single and homogeneous heaven."[2]

Modern man, who from his school days has assimilated elements of a rationalistic-mechanistic world view, will have difficulty imagining reality as an ordered, living, harmonious Cosmos.[3] Our understanding of the world contains far fewer visible, figurative components, and the idea of an extra-human nature, pervaded by vital principles, goals, and values, is in general alien to us. Moreover, the contemporary picture of the world is fragmentary. It is made up of disassociated bits of knowledge and opinions that fit together very poorly, coming from different scientific disciplines and domains of culture. For example, those parts of the picture of the world that are formed on the basis of physics and astronomy "fit" in far from all respects with the notions of the biological sciences about the world. In turn, psychology or history places man in his own world, which is not at all like the world described by natural science. Moreover, all of this knowledge and these opinions frequently change, which perhaps is good for keeping a culture dynamic, but at the same time it certainly leaves many people without convincing answers to questions as to why the world was created and what the meaning of human life is.

The integral and harmonious Cosmos of antiquity did not contain all these divisions. There were no fixed boundaries between nature and society: man was an inseparable part of the universal cosmic process. And he really did feel himself to be a "microcosm" in which the multitude of cosmic connections, forces, and elements are intertwined and through which they pass.

The spiritualization of the Cosmos

What happened to the ancient understanding of the Cosmos later in history? It suffered its first profound transformation in the Middle Ages, in a new social and spiritual context defined by the hegemony of the Christian religion. However, some basic features of the way the ancients understood the world were preserved in this context as well. The Cosmos of Thomas Aquinas and the Cosmos of Dante quite legitimately derive their origins from the Cosmos of Plato and Aristotle. It is no accident that the latter was the supreme authority in the epoch of medieval scholastic scholarship. But the ancient image of a closed, self-sufficient Cosmos was substantially spiritualized by the constant presence and action of the creative Divine forces and principles that transcended it. The cosmic elements increasingly were losing their self-sufficiency and were becoming the material shells of spiritual forces.

The world came to be represented as merely the visible embodiment of Divine providence. It was the constant action of Divine prototypes that supported the Cosmos, and without these nonmaterial idea-forces it would turn into chaos, formless matter without qualities. Like Aristotle's forms, these idea-prototypes were embodied in things, thus imparting to them their qualities—properties to inorganic things, vital force to plants, a soul to animals, and so forth.

The Middle Ages preserved and even strengthened the ancient idea of the correspondence between the world and man, between the macrocosm and the microcosm. Since man was created "in the image of God," then in his rational soul he became like a part of Divine reason, while in his body, which consisted of all the elements, he became like the Universe. Hence he is a "microcosm" resembling the "macrocosm," and, conversely, the Cosmos as a whole displays a likeness to man in its structure and functioning. Consequently, much of what is said in the Holy Scriptures about the creation of heaven is metaphorically applicable to man. And what is known about the relation between man's body and man's soul is applicable, metaphorically, symbolically, to cosmic life—after all, the entire world is an envelope of the same Divine logos, a bit of which each finds in himself as well.

The purposes and possibilities of cognition are understood in accordance with this overall picture of the structure of the world. A study of the material, sensuous world is not regarded as an end in itself; it is only a step toward the contemplation of the suprasensory prototypes hidden behind it. Thus the visible world in all its manifestations is testimony to the mysteries of the invisible world—the starry heavens are, for example, nothing other than the metaphorical language of Divine revelation. Hence the constant temptation to astrological activities, alchemy, magic, and interpretations of nature as a Book in which is embodied in symbolic form a content that the Holy Scriptures gives to people in another form.

As a result of this spiritualization, the Cosmos, the harmony and self-sufficient beauty of which was the delight of the thinkers of antiquity, became increasingly a reflection of religious and moral truths and a unique machine for the ruin and salvation of the human soul, thereby illustrating in cosmological terms the Christian doctrine of human destiny.

Obviously such an interpretation of the Cosmos opened up abundant opportunities for multifarious forms of mysticism and magical practices, restrained only by orthodox faith and the canons of medieval university scholarship. This was especially evident in the late Middle Ages, when, as a result of the crisis of scholasticism and the spirit of the Renaissance, an entire bouquet of unorthodox religious and intellectual sects and currents burst forth. Demonology, alchemy, astrology, natural magic, the cabala, and various kinds of "grass-roots" magical practices (witchcraft, sorcery, the art of prophecy, etc.) emerged onto the surface of culture, creating a bizarre spiritual atmosphere in which scholasticism disappeared while modern European scientific thought was born. Man as a "microcosm" was literally dissolved in the fantastical pulsations of cosmic elements and forces, sympathies and antipathies. Jacob Boehme, [H.C.] Agrippa, Paracelsus, Robert Fludd, John Dee, Tommaso Campanella, and many other mystics and "natural magi" who created this atmosphere attempted at the same time to use it as a framework for elaborating new techniques, unknown to the Middle Ages, of acting upon nature, especially human nature—on man's body, his health, his feelings, and his reason.

Was the Cosmos totally "destroyed"?

It is usually assumed that the conception of the Cosmos receded entirely into the past as a result of the scientific and general cultural revolution in Europe in the sixteenth and seventeenth centuries. Hundreds of works in the history of science and in philosophy have been written about this revolution in world view. Alexandre Koyré, the famous historian of science, expressed this revolution in the vivid image of "the destruction of the Cosmos." "The destruction of the Cosmos and, as a result, the disappearance from science of all the arguments based on this concept"[4] was the principal feature of the modern European intellectual revolution, which led to the elaboration of the modern rational understanding of the world. "The disintegration of the Cosmos," adds Koyré, "is in my view the most revolutionary upheaval that human reason has accomplished (or suffered) since the invention of the Cosmos by the ancient Greeks."[5]

The complex hierarchical structure of the Cosmos, with its "sublunar" and "superlunar" worlds, spheres of planets and stars, the cycle of the cosmic elements, and the play of divine and demonic forces, was replaced by a new scientific picture of the world: homogeneous and infinite, governed by universal mechanical laws of the Universe, in which there was no longer a place for any kind of cosmic influences, "sympathies," or "antipathies." Aside from this, there was no haven in the new Universe for all of those spiritual beings—angels and demons, astral spirits and archae—that filled the medieval Cosmos in abundance.

The Cosmos was dislodged as the dominant world-view construct. That is incontestable. But can one say that it totally disappeared from spiritual culture? In my view, this is not the case. Even in science, a "cosmic" understanding of the world did not recede entirely into the past. It was relegated to the background, it became marginal, but even in such form it continued to serve as an efficacious source for various parascientific and some scientific constructs.

Clear traces of the influence of "cosmism" are to be found, for example, in Goethe's doctrine of nature, especially his theory of color, which was formulated as an alternative to Newton's mechanical-geometric optics. Similarly, the German natural philosophy of Schelling, Hegel, Oken, and others contains a multitude of cosmic metaphors and restores the language of cosmic elements and qualities that already had been quite forgotten by the beginning of the nineteenth century.

The cosmism of Russian natural scientists and philosophers of the late nineteenth and early twentieth centuries—N.F. Fedorov, N.A. Morozov, K.E. Tsiolkovskii, A.L. Chizhevskii, and others—was a vivid and curious phenomenon. Their ideas about the joint evolution of the cosmos, the biosphere, and human society and their doctrines of cosmic nature and the cosmic destiny of man clearly did not fit into the standard canons of science. The scientific community looked at them as eccentrics and "heretics" engaged in mystical visionary activities, restoring astrological studies, and such things.

It must be admitted that such assessments were not groundless. Take, for example, A.L. Chizhevskii's statement, which unambiguously testifies to his "pre-Galilean" intuitions:

> When the Pythagoreans were devising their theory of the "harmony of the spheres" on the basis of elementary notions of the movement of the planets, they were not even able to imagine how lawful the movements of

the planets actually were and how keen yet firm was the bond of the planets in all the manifestations of their physical life. Just as physiologists find in living organisms a connection among their several organs, a *consensus partium* whereby the different parts are regulated and coordinated by the nervous and circulatory systems, so astronomers in their turn, studying phenomena in the Solar system, discover in it phenomena analogous to the functions of the living organism.[6]

Of course historians of science have quite a number of examples of scientific conceptions being born under the influence of various unorthodox ideas. Chizhevskii's heliobiology is precisely one of these. Moreover, he himself, of course, considered himself to be not an astrologer[7] but an authentic scientist, penetrating into the secrets of complex and confused phenomena, which the science contemporaneous with him had disregarded owing to its being dominated by mechanistic views and the disciplinary partitions separating biology, the social sciences, and astrophysical studies. What is important for us here is only the fact that intuitions of the Cosmos are alive in the science of the twentieth century as well and that they can be mobilized and can grow into interesting constructions, albeit deviating somewhat from the standards of ordinary science.

"Cosmic consciousness": Psychological aspects

Many people evidently assume that a penchant for a mystical perception of the world and belief in magical connections is the lot of some sort of selected representatives of the human species—magicians and sorcerers, practitioners of black magic and visionaries, prophets and poets. But such a perception is much more widespread, and indeed in principle it is alien to no man. If it were otherwise, these aspects of human experience would hardly be so stable and would hardly become so widespread among so many people at certain times, as, for example, nowadays in our country.

There is a multitude of data indicating that the roots of such phenomena reside in forms and methods of interpreting the world that lie deep, driven into the subconscious. These levels of consciousness are latent in an adult civilized person living in a rationally constructed urban environment, and he has virtually no reflective access to them. However, this does not mean that they do not operate or that they cannot be mobilized in unusual or dramatic situations or in certain collective actions of people. Anthropologists and specialists in the comparative study of the thought of people of different cultures all agree that considerable vestiges of "paleothinking" are preserved among representatives of European civilization and that, irrespective of their level of education, people in principle are not protected against regressions to this type of thinking, especially in extraordinary situations. A specialist in this area noted:

> Even without considering such states of consciousness as sleep, the normal person does not always function in one and the same regime of mental activity. His mentality from the genetic point of view is not one and the same when he is in a distracted state and when he is attentive and concentrated. It changes when a person moves from rational scientific or practical activity to the emotional perception of people or of some events. One can say that mental life has different starting points. At one time a person behaves "primitively," and at another he becomes relatively "cultured" and "civilized." Generally speaking, the psychology of development demonstrates that archaic types of behavior not only occur in the normal adult in certain extraordinary situations but are constantly present as a basis of the whole of his mental structure and are vitally important in this capacity for the functioning of higher forms of mentality.[8]

The rational forms and levels of thinking are not separated, in either their historical or their personal dimensions, by any impassable gaps or boundaries from "paleothinking." It is another matter that the latter is usually not manifested either in language or in people's judgments or inferences. Archaic forms of thinking are mute and subconscious. They are embodied in bodily actions, in affects, in the concrete symbolism of life. A person may conform to the modern rational picture of the world in his rationalistic activity and in his logically regulated judgments, whereas his intuitive perception of the world, his bodily incorporation into the surrounding environment, his eye, finally, might conform to another type of perception of the world, including the one that ancient thinkers succeeded in expressing as experiencing the world as a living Cosmos responding to human actions.[9]

But perhaps the human consciousness can still be "torn away" from its dark archaic roots, these sources of mythopoeic, cosmic, occult, and similar ideas? The findings of contemporary neuropsychology tell us that this is hardly possible. Working against it is above all the fundamental fact of the interhemispherical asymmetry of the human brain. The left hemisphere (in most people, who are right-handed) is responsible for rational thinking, which operates with words. The right hemisphere, on the other hand, works without words, without logical consistency—intuitively. It is responsible for the emotional-figurative perception of the surrounding environment, the instantaneous recognition of the faces of other people, and the recognition of voices and melodies; it grasps, finally, the integral "physiognomy" of being. It is extremely difficult to interfere in the work of the right hemisphere or even to feel it and follow it (in the same way as we can control our speech or logical arguments). The well-known astrophysicist Carl Sagan, who looked at the evolution of human reason in the context of the evolution of the Earth, very graphically pointed out this difficulty. The capacity to feel and in some way to utilize the work of the right hemisphere is like the ability to see stars on a sunny day. "When the sun sets, we are able to perceive the stars. In the same way, the brilliance of our most recent evolutionary accretions, the verbal abilities of the left hemisphere, obscures our awareness of the intuitive right hemisphere, which in our ancestors must have been the principal means of perceiving the world."[10]

The coexistence of these two in many respects incommensurate ways of becoming aware of things helps us to understand why many things seem to us to have a double aspect. On the one hand, we know, for example, that the Moon is a huge dead rock flying in a void according to the laws of mechanics; on the other hand, the intuitive layers of our psyche, which are not under the control of our ego, "recognize" the Moon in its mythological features—in the mysterious and efficacious influences it has on the most diverse aspects of human life.

A belief in astrology, UFOs, extrasensory phenomena, and so forth is rooted to no small degree in their consonance with this "right-hemisphere" type of consciousness and its specific "logic" of connecting phenomena and things with one another. As Sagan writes, "These are by and large, if I may use the phrase, limbic and right-hemisphere doctrines, dream protocols, natural—the word is certainly perfectly appropriate—and human responses to the complexity of the environment we inhabit. But they are also mystical and occult doctrines, devised in such a way that they are not subject to disproof and characteristically impervious to rational discussion."[11]

One other very important feature of "cosmic consciousness" is that reality appears in it as something living and emotionally colored, responding to man's expectations and prophecies—put more succinctly, not as an objective, alienated, and soulless "it" but as a living and responsive "thou." Once again, the data of psychology and anthropology tell us that such a personal, "physiognomic" perception genetically precedes a purely objective perception of things. In the very first days of life, when infants still do not perceive things as such, they are prepared to perceive smiling or frowning faces and whole situations as favorable or as alarming, as threatening them. Some psychologists think that such schemata of perceiving the world are innate in man.[12] Whether this is so or not, what is initial in the development of a child and in the evolution of collective human thought in the perception of the world and its cosmic elements and forces (earth, water, fire, wind, lightning, etc.) is their empathetic, personal experience, an attitude toward them as something living, animate, as a "thou."

> The people of antiquity, like modern savages as well, always regarded nature as part of society and society as included in nature and dependent on cosmic forces. For them nature and man are not in opposition to one another, and hence there should not be two correspondingly different methods of cognition. . . . This does not mean (as people often think) that primitive man invested the inanimate world with human characteristics to explain natural phenomena. For primitive man, the inanimate world simply does not exist.[13]

Of course, what we have said does not mean that "cosmic consciousness"—feeling oneself to be a small part of a powerful and mysterious cycle of cosmic elements—is easily articulated by modern man. Another understanding of the world is dominant today. However, as a latent, rudimentary stratum, it is not alien to us and could burst through to the surface in the guise of diverse symbols of consciousness and also of such states as a person experiences when seized by a feeling of unity with the world, of relating to it as to a living powerful partner—a good one or a bad one, a menacing one or a peaceful one, and so forth.

The magic of the Earth: The folk Cosmos

Elements of a cosmic perception of the world would hardly have been preserved and continue to elicit a response in the consciousness of many people if their influence were limited merely to refined mystical doctrines. However, the reasons for the persistence and vitality of the language of "cosmic forces and elements" lie not only in the theoretical doctrines— usually esoteric and accessible to relatively few. In addition to these factors and the psychological premises we have just examined, a cosmic perception of the world has deep roots in traditional, folk agrarian experience and the associated practices of folk medicine, dwelling construction, and traditional crafts and technologies.

The close ties between the cosmological constructions of antiquity and folk agrarian experience have been noted by many investigators. For example, A.V. Akhutin, in his profound comparative study of the science of antiquity and modern European science, evaluates this source of ancient cosmologies as follows:

> There can be no question of there being any contrivance or arbitrary speculation. Stones, trees, animals, and the heavenly bodies; the climate and the character of the locality, the nature of winds, waters, and earth, the customs of the inhabitants; the cycle of rural work, determined by the succession of seasons of the year, the eternal rotation of heavenly bodies—in a word, the entire cosmic household, to an experienced "physician" [*fisiolog*]

and "wise man" knowing its eternal structure, is a direct experience and an empirically verifiable speculation. . . . A peasant knows from experience the "nature" of his crops, fruit trees, animals, winds, waters, soils, and the seasonal weather. . . . It is not difficult to see that the understanding of nature in antiquity (the indivisible internal principle determining the growth, character, habits, and abilities of some "being"), as well as the understanding of the Cosmos in antiquity (an eternally reproducing order of a whole that is complete in itself) is imposed by agrarian "works and days."[14]

There are stable and multifarious ties between the dominant forms of people's production and lives and those cosmological structures that a particular epoch produces. It is no accident that in all traditional societies, where people's way of life and their work rhythm are an organic part of the cycle of the natural elements, there are structurally similar mythopoeic and philosophical pictures of the Cosmos.

An extremely important foundation of this similarity is the notion of the primary principles, the basic elements out of which the Cosmos is formed— earth, water, air, and fire. In some cultures, wood, metal, or, as in the Indo-Tibetan culture, space, a more abstract primary element, were added. The very idea of first principles goes back deep in history and is evidently archetypal for human consciousness. The language of these elements is seemingly eternal and universal—it is intelligible both to a child and to an illiterate person, and, on the other hand, it is capable, thanks to the extremely rich symbolism inherent in it, of expressing subtle metaphysical ideas.

Why have these seemingly quite naive notions about the cosmic elements established themselves so firmly and universally in human culture? It is undoubtedly a question of their real significance in people's everyday life, especially those who are part of traditional agrarian production. In this sphere, the earth and water, fire and air do not at all present themselves in those simple physical and chemical properties in which science describes them. Let us take water, for example. This is a truly universal condition of human life. Water quenches thirst; it is an ingredient in the majority of foods; it is nourishing moisture for the plants man grows; people have traditionally settled around water; it is also the means and symbol of purity and coolness, and so on and so forth. It is therefore understandable that water is perceived in popular consciousness as living and responsive, requiring care and respect. In many images and symbols, this life of the aqueous element and its participation in human affairs are reflected in people's language and mythopoeic views.[15]

The earth-element has still greater scope in the collective consciousness. It is one of the most saturated images people use to express their understanding of the world. It is both the soil, which man cultivates and on which he lives, and the substratum, which feeds everything living and to which this living thing returns again after completing its life cycle. It is both the local landscape surrounding man, where he was born and where he lives, as well as the planet as a whole. The unbounded possibilities of the earth are associated above all with the generative, productive force of this element. That force is the "great mother-earth"—a universal mythologem, found in all agrarian civilizations. Simultaneously with this role as the foundation, the bosom of human life, the earth is understood as an ethical principle,[16] and in its supreme, mystical dimension it is a "god-earth" as that which is ready to receive the Divine prototypes and be transformed into god-man.

Hence it is quite natural that the spheres of "high," intellectualized mysticism were often "nourished" and came into contact with the "grass-roots" sacral-magical formulas of agrarian experience. Let us take one, comparatively recent example. The founder of anthroposophy, the Austrian philosopher and mystic Rudolf Steiner, combining various mystical and mysterious doctrines of the West and the East, made it his goal to draw the human soul out of the circle of petty illusory impressions and "to immerse it in the natural Cosmic element." Alongside the theoretical treatises on this matter (one of which has a name that is classical for this genre, *Macrocosmos and Microcosmos* [Makrokosmos i mikrokosmos]), Steiner also had a number of practically oriented programs. One of these had to do with agrarian practices. Not long before his death, in 1924, he summed it up in a course of lectures entitled *Agriculture* [Agrikul'tura], which he gave to his closest disciples. In it he warned that the ever-growing penetration into agriculture of machine technology, chemistry, biology, and other sciences is causing the farmer to lose his profound connections with "mother-earth." Steiner called on his disciples to help peasants preserve and restore these ties with the "great life of the Cosmos" and with the "physical and spiritual forces of the Earth"—connections forgotten by contemporary scholars, who regard the earth as a laboratory object. Steiner taught that it was necessary to create, together with the peasants but without the scientists, "a genuine people's agriculture" in which the mystical-organic perception of nature would be combined with "biodynamic methods" of working the soil that develop traditional agrarian technologies and exclude the use of inorganic fertilizers, poisonous chemicals, and so forth. Incidentally, these ideas were not forgotten and were implemented in the program of the "organic agricultural movement," which exists in Austria and some other countries.

In addition to the farming experience in the narrow sense, the peasant home and the entire life cycle of the farmer from earliest infancy to old age and death are "cosmic." Methods of folk medicine, which are growing in popularity today, acquire a meaning only in the structure of a cosmic understanding of the world. Thus, the traditional peasant home is an unconscious modeling of the Cosmos in its structure. It is no more arbitrary than a bird's nest or the hives of wild bees. In a Russian peasant home, the hearth-stove as the center of the dwelling, the chamber, the cellar, the grain, the sauna, the external decorations—all these things grow organically from the cosmic elements, stand outside the rapid events of cultural change, and correspond to the "eternal," cosmic style of peasant labor and everyday life. The principal techniques and prescriptions of folk medicine are also associated with such a world-perception of the immersion of man in the organic cycle of the elements. It becomes clear why practically everything that surrounds mankind possesses healing properties: grasses, flowers and grains, milk and the blood of animals, various minerals and resins, dirt, and vapors. In all systems of folk medicine, healing power is ascribed both to the elements themselves and to their qualities (earth and water, air and fire, cold and heat) in their "pure form"—after all, not only the surrounding world but man himself is woven out of them.

* * *

Contemporary man shows himself to be divorced from the cosmic principles of existence and increasingly immersed in the rational-technical environment that he himself created and in a self-sufficient world of social relations with no ties to nature. There is something abnormal in this disintegration of being, and hence it is the natural reaction of many people to search for more integral forms of spiritual experience and to experience a growing mistrust of one-sidedly rational orientations of life and culture. The cosmic understanding of the world, backed by the intuitions of ancient and medieval learning, of mysticism, and of many philosophical systems, opens up great possibilities for such quests. However, for those who assume that this understanding of the world leads to some as-yet unknown, "advanced" types of experience, it is worth bearing in mind that behind these quests, as a rule, there are backward-looking movements of thought. In spite of the seeming (to modern man) abstractness and triviality of the present-day noncosmic perception of the world, the latter is the result of the long critical elaboration of the antecedent intellectual culture, and in this sense it is internally more complex and richer than one or another form of "cosmic consciousness."

Notes

1. It should be pointed out at once that the words 'cosmos' and 'cosmic' have no relation here to contemporary cosmonautics. The latter is constructed in accordance with the laws of the "extracosmic" world of contemporary science, and, moreover, it involves the transfer of terrestrial laboratories over comparatively short distances into extraterrestrial space.

2. Plato, *Sochineniia v trekh tomakh* (Moscow, 1971), vol. 3, pt. 1, p. 541.

3. This does not mean that there are no exceptions here. For various reasons, some of which will be mentioned below, the cosmic perception of the world has not died even in the twentieth century. It was characteristic, for example, of representatives of Russian philosophical-scientific cosmism. Does not this thought, for example, sound "Platonic": "The Cosmos engendered not evil and error but the reason and happiness of all that exists. To understand this, we need only move to a higher point of view: to imagine the future of the Earth and to embrace with our reason the infinitude of the Universe or at least our own Milky Way. Then we will see that the cosmos is like a supremely good and supremely rational animal" (K.E. Tsiolkovskii, *Grezy o zemle i nebe* [Tula, 1986], p. 311).

4. A. Koyré, *Ocherki istorii filosofskoi mysli* (Moscow, 1985), p. 130.

5. Ibid., p. 131.

6. A.L. Chizhevskii, *Zemnoe ekho solnechnykh bur'* (Moscow, 1973), pp. 82–83 (*consensus partium* is Latin for agreement of the parts).

7. But Chizhevskii was not averse to toying with such terminology. Thus, in 1926–27 he published the articles "Contemporary Astrology" [Sovremennaia astrologiia], "The Astrology of the Future" [Astrologiia budushchego], "Astrology of Our Days" [Astrologiia nashikh dnei] (not yet suspecting what this would later become), in which he noted an analogy between his own investigations and the current in astrology that was involved with predicting mass events, such as, for example, epidemics, wars, earthquakes, and so forth.

8. H. Werner, *Comparative Psychology of Mental Development* (New York, 1948), p. 4.

9. Here is one curious fact. American psychologists decided to clarify what understanding of physical phenomena (various movements, transformations of matter, etc.) a person adhered to in his practical everyday life. It turned out that for the vast majority of people (with the exception of a few physicists who were specialists) in their life experience there "forms some consistent intuitive theory of movement that contradicts the basic laws of Newtonian mechanics. . . . This theory is surprisingly similar to the pre-Newtonian theory of impetus or 'acquired force' " (M. McCloskey, "Intuitivnaia fizika," *V mire nauki*, 1983, no. 6, pp. 90–91). The theory of impetus is a medieval conception that is entirely within the framework of Aristotelian mechanics, which in turn has meaning only in the above-described construction of the Cosmos. Thus we find that a person's head may contain information acquired in school about the Galilean-Newtonian universe, but his eyes and hands act as if he were placed in the Cosmos of antiquity.

10. Carl Sagan, *The Dragons of Eden: Speculations on the Evolution of Human Intelligence* (New York: Random House, 1977), pp. 168–69.

11. Ibid., p. 238.

12. See U. Naisser, *Poznanie i real'nost'. Smysl i perspektivy kognitivnoi psikhologii* (Moscow, 1981), p. 201.

13. G. Frankfort et al., *V preddverii filosofii* (Moscow, 1984), pp. 25–26.

14. A.V. Akhutin, *Poniatie "priroda" v antichnosti i v Novoe vremia ("fiusis" i "natura")* (Moscow, 1988), pp. 166, 168.

15. Water is "little sister" and "healer," "living" and the "blood of the earth," and so forth. Language reflects the special value of sources of water: *"rodnik"* [source], *"kladez'"* [fount], *"kliuch"* [spring]. As with other elements, a vast stratum of popular consciousness is associated with it (see, for example, A.N. Afanas′ev, *Zhivaia voda i veshchee slovo* [Moscow, 1988]).

16. This is very characteristic of peasant consciousness, which saw a danger for its own moral underpinnings in man's divorce from the earth. F.M. Dostoevskii expressed this ethical-cosmic role of the earth in his *Diary of a Writer* [Dnevnik pisatelia]: "A nation should in its vast majority be born and sprout on the earth, on the soil on which grain and trees grow.... The earth and the soil contain something sacramental. If you want to have mankind be reborn to something better, almost to make human beings out of beasts, then grant them the earth and you will achieve your goal" (*Polnoe sobranie sochinenii* [Moscow, 1981], vol. 23, pp. 96, 98).

I.A. BESKOVA

The Nature of Transpersonal Experience

The history of human culture records diverse notions about possible forms of existence of the soul or analogous substances after the disintegration of the corporeal shell. Even where investigators of primitive cultures conclude that some community is at such a low level of development that it has elaborated no ideas concerning the existence of gods, demons, spirits, and so forth—even there, a cautious attitude toward such evidence is necessary. Actually, the conviction that "savages" do not have such beliefs may be less a reflection of the real state of affairs than, let us say, the reluctance of members of that community to familiarize Europeans with elements of their culture that bear on spheres of life activity that are most meaningful for the tribe. Thus the anthropologist W.R. Trevathan[1] mentions particular difficulties arising from attempts to study the actions and rituals associated with the birth of a child (as well as the stages directly preceding and following this event). Even where there is a friendly attitude toward the investigator, there still remain spheres of life to which representatives of the tribe were reluctant to allow Europeans access. For example, there is the well-known case where one anthropologist, who had lost hope of "officially" learning about the character of the rituals accompanying the birth of an infant, attempted to sneak a look at what was happening in the hut. This curiosity almost cost him his life, despite the recent goodwill of his host.

It is perfectly obvious that just as important for a community as the mystery of birth is the mystery of death and of all the subsequent transformations befalling a person or what is recognized to be his remains. And, although a simple sifting through a culture is not sufficient to conclude that such beliefs are universal, that conclusion does seem to follow from certain

Russian text © 1994 by the Presidium of the Russian Academy of Sciences. "O prirode transpersonal'nogo opyta," *Voprosy filosofii*, 1994, no. 2, pp. 35–44. A publication of the Institute of Philosophy, Russian Academy of Sciences.

Irina Aleksandrovna Beskova is a Doctor of Philosophical Sciences and a senior research associate at the Institute of Philosophy, Russian Academy of Sciences.

more general theoretical propositions whose validity we shall attempt briefly to substantiate.

The question, specifically, concerns the role a system of beliefs (as primitive as you may wish) plays in securing favorable conditions for the life activity of the members of a community. In this regard, some approaches developed within the framework of sociobiological studies are not without interest. Usually, in examining questions having to do with identifying the place and role of beliefs in the life of communities, cultural and cognitive aspects are accented, while less attention is given to those aspects of the problem that might pinpoint some of the underlying dependencies between the state and development of the gene pool of a population and the functioning in the community of certain systems of ideas constituting the basis of its culture. But both aspects of the problem deserve attention. For example, the "biological advantages" of certain kinds of prohibitions are quite well known. Thus the taboo on marriages between blood relatives substantially lowers the risk of possible duplication of the genetic flaws of one parent and thereby eliminates a vital factor leading to the gradual degeneration of the community.

Somewhat less obvious relations are found in the regulation of mental life. Indeed, one of the ways to reduce anxiety (a very strong negative factor influencing man's adaptive capabilities) is to reveal the external source of anxiety, which, even though it may be illusory, will nonetheless enable one to say to oneself: "My problems have to do with such-and-such. And since I know this, I am able to avoid unpleasant problems by eliminating the revealed causes." As a consequence, certain limitations of his own behavior enable the individual to expunge the factor of anxiety from his consciousness or at least reduce the extent of its influence.[2]

Thus it would seem that taboos, strictly formulated prohibitions, provide a certain psychological compensation in the form of reduced anxiety and increased self-confidence, precisely by virtue of the subject's becoming aware of certain limitations on behavior and actions: "I will not violate the prohibitions, and hence I will not bring down upon myself the wrath of the gods."

This, of course, does not exhaust the range of the psychotherapeutic influence of various forms of beliefs on the state of a community as a whole as well as of its individual members. For example, faith that an appeal, properly composed and in ritual form, to a totem will bring the desired result gives a person confidence in practical affairs and enables him to keep hope alive in difficult life situations. This is very important, since such emotions as fear or lack of confidence not only reduce the probability of a quick and appropriate response under conditions of a constantly changing environment but also place stressful pressure on the individual. As we know, in a state of stress, the reproductive function suffers first, so that individuals that are most subject to stress leave fewer progeny than their better-adapted fellows. But since a state of stress (or, more accurately, distress) involves negative emotions such as fear, lack of confidence, and anxiety, the mitigation of which can be promoted by a community's active system of beliefs, the capacity to believe, which increases resistance to stress factors, proves to be a selectively valuable quality.

Some conclusions of sociobiologists can be presented in support of this point. Thus, E.O. Wilson assumed that certain forms of beliefs will be preserved and propagated in a community if they help to improve a person's adaptive capabilities. On the other hand, if some beliefs weaken the survivability and productivity of those who hold them, then, despite their possible emotional attractiveness, they will disappear in the course of evolution. According to Wilson, this process is genetically determined, since genes determine the functioning of man's nervous and hormonal systems and the work of his sense organs and hence almost certainly influence learning processes. Certain restrictions on the development of certain types of activity and behavior are engendered. As a result, the selection of ideas and beliefs is influenced by a chain of interrelations that ascend from the genetic level through the physiological to the structures of individual and group learning.[3]

Since situations associated with death or birth are important for any community of human beings, it may be assumed that corresponding systems of beliefs will be formed in all cultures. Such universality does not, of course, mean that these systems must be all alike. Indeed, they can be very different, and their rational reconstruction can be quite difficult for a number of reasons. In endeavoring to interpret cultures far removed from us in time, we inevitably and most often unconsciously impose upon them stereotypes of perception and interpretation from our own time. It is very difficult to avoid this transference, since it is essential to know that some proposition perceived as indisputable is in fact limited by the framework of a particular culture. But this knowledge already implicitly presupposes that a prior adequate appraisal of the culture the investigator is trying to understand already exists. The upshot is that, to evaluate correctly the phenomena of a culture quite remote from us, it is necessary to know how one should evaluate these phenomena; in order not to impose the stereotypes of a later view of the world on our interpretation of early cultures, it is necessary to know what components are the acquisition of the later forms of development of human life activity.

This task is internally contradictory in many respects. That is why rational reconstructions of the processes of the formation and functioning of any structures of the past are so difficult. But one cannot say that such reconstructions are in principle impossible.

Taking these considerations into account, we shall attempt to examine those aspects of transpersonal experience that have to do with the themes of human death, the transmigration of souls, and regression into deeply archaic layers of experience. First let us note that different cultures have formed different notions of the existence of the soul after death and the fate awaiting it. Some of them are extremely cruel, even cruel for the souls undergoing trial, causing them infinite torment if they fail and leaving almost no hope (if any) for salvation. Others are astonishingly humane: in them there is no rigor of judgment over the "inept" or deeply sin-laden soul. The narration, rather, contains notes of compassion and an obvious desire to help the soul, insofar as this is possible, to avoid falling into deeper layers of worlds after death in which the trials the soul must undergo increase in number and in cruelty.

The Tibetan *Book of the Dead*,[4] which was compiled as a kind of guide to enable the soul to move through the labyrinths of existence after death as successfully as possible, is very interesting in this regard. The potential failures the soul may suffer along the way are not so much an incentive to further condemnation as a basis for a call to concentrate and to make use of the smallest chances to improve one's subsequent fate. For example, the following fragment is instructive:

CHIKHAI BARDO[5] is the Bardo of the Hour of Death. The first stage. . . . Soon you will breathe your last breath, and it will stop. Now you will see the Primary Clear Light. An incredible expanse, boundless like an ocean without waves under a cloudless sky, will open up before you.

You will float like a feather, free, alone.

Do not be distracted, do not rejoice! Do not be afraid! This is the world of your death!

Take advantage of death, for it is a great opportunity. Preserve the clarity of your thoughts, do not cloud them even with suffering. . . .

Collect yourself, seek the Primary Light with your gaze. When you espy it, receive it. "There it is!" cry out. Do not allow your attention to wander aimlessly. This is a meeting directly with ultimate truth, the Law (Dharma Kāya). You will be able to see, to recognize—you will become what you in fact are. You will discover the secret, you will discover the trials of Life and Death, you yourself will become this Light. This is the Perpendicular Path, accessible to the few. . . . The second stage. You have not seen the Primary Clear Light. In the antechamber to the next Bardo, the Second Clear Light may begin to gleam before you. Look at it! If you are able to see it, to name it, and to accept the Second Light of the first moment of death, you will avoid much that is to come. When you see it—say the name of your favorite Deity. Cry out: "Lord! Is this you?!" . . .

If we have not recognized, if we have not seen the Light, at this point we may meet the Sentries of Eternity in any guise. These are helpers, the Great Figures of Union with that same Primary Light. If you have not seen the Light but have regained consciousness, collected yourself, and know where you are, hold this one thought in your head—humility! Whomever you meet, bow and remember at least some prayer from your past life, at least something in which you believed . . .

CHÖNYID BARDO is the Bardo of Karmic Illusions.

Even if you have not regained consciousness, you have fallen under the Primary Light that flashed from all directions into Chikhai Bardo. Now you will emerge with a consciousness separated from the flesh you no longer need in the Chönyid Bardo.

Be watchful and attentive! Do not hurry! Do not be afraid! You have died. Understand this and do not grasp onto what has passed, do not irritate your feelings, do not let them have free play and swallow you. Waves of feelings may carry us away into terrible places. Collect yourself and look around you with an attentive and kind gaze. The Light will poise itself before you, like a bright mirage, playful and blinding. Within the Light you will hear thunder, like the clapping of thousands of gigantic hands. These are the sounds of the ultimate Essence. Do not take fright! Nothing can harm you, for you do not exist! Hence you can become whatever you wish. Become this sound, respond to it. These mirages are you, yourself! He who does not exist contains in himself all and nothing! If you do not recognize and do not respond to the visions and the sounds, if you do not espy yourself and yours in them, fear will seize you!

You will fall into other worlds of true misfortunes and torments as through ice that has broken up. Be on your guard against involuntary feelings. Let the good-hearted hardness of the pure glass of a mirror be your main sensation.[6]

As we see, in this fragment the soul is a wanderer capable of exerting an active influence on the nature of its subsequent fate. The very ideas of the nature of the soul also varied. But most often it was understood as a substance animating the human body and capable of leaving it, both forever and for a short time (in sleep, during grave illnesses, etc.). In some cultures, man was thought to have several souls, some of which leave his body after death while others remain not far away and can wander about the burial place, causing mischief to the living. Accordingly, rituals were developed aimed at protecting those left alive from orphaned souls. The spectrum of actions in these rituals was very wide—from rather crude and categorical actions (for example, when the floor was swept carefully after a banquet with the words, "Souls, you have eaten and drunk, now get away!" or when the opening in the walls of the hut through which the deceased was borne away was filled up so that the soul could not find its way back) to milder forms with elements of precaution (thus, the peasants of Pomerania left straw from the funeral hearse near fresh graves so that the soul could sit down and rest and not harass the living).

Some peoples recognized several kinds of soul: material, vegetable, animal, and human. Accordingly, the transmigration of a soul after death from its vehicle into other substances was possible.

Perhaps the idea of the transmigration of souls received its most finished forms in the conception of Samsāra—continuous rebirth, the cycling of lives. As we know, this doctrine was based on the idea of kinship among all living things. Hence death is not a transition from existence to nonexistence but only a change in the form of existence, in its external shell. The next birth is possible not only in the guise of a human being but also as an animal or a plant. What it would be was determined by karma—the aggregate of actions by the living being in conjunction with the consequences of the acts it had committed. Karma determines not only the present conditions of a being's existence—health or illness, poverty or wealth, happiness or unhappiness, duration of life, social status, and so forth—but also the prospects of progressing toward the ultimate goal: a liberation from the fetters of profane existence and the possibility of breaking out of the circle of endless rebirths.

Do these and similar beliefs have any real foundations, do they reflect, even symbolically, something that actually happens with a person in the process of phylogeny and ontogeny, or are these purely speculative constructions with only a cultural-historical (for the nonbeliever) or a religious-mystical value? Should we, from the standpoint of our present knowledge about the world, simply put aside such ideas, or does it make sense nonetheless to look attentively at ancient tradition and attempt to use the information it contains for a deeper understanding of the nature of consciousness and of the distinctive features of man's perception and thought?

Let us try to analyze these problems from the second viewpoint. First let us direct our attention to the fact that phenomena consonant with ancient notions of the after-death existence of souls are revealed in some studies of altered states of consciousness, as for example, in studying the transformations of consciousness that occur as the result of the use of psychedelics and hallucinogens. Here is how Stanislav Grof and Joan Halifax describe the experience of patients during psychedelic sessions:

> The common denominator of this otherwise rich and ramified group is the individual's feeling that his or her consciousness has expanded beyond the usual ego boundaries and has transcended the limitations of time and space. In "normal" or usual state of consciousness, individuals experience themselves as existing within the boundaries of the physical body (the body image), and their perception of the environment is restricted by the physically determined range of the exteroceptors. Both internal perception (interoception) and perception of the environment (exteroception) are confined within

the usual space-time boundaries. Under ordinary circumstances individuals vividly perceive their present situation and their immediate environment; they recall past events and anticipate the future or fantasize about it. In transpersonal experiences occurring in psychedelic sessions, one or several of the above limitations appear to be transcended. In some instances individuals experience loosening of their usual ego boundaries; their consciousness and self-awareness seem to expand to include and encompass other people as well as elements of the external world. They can also continue experiencing their own identities, but at a different time, in a different place, or in a different context. In yet other cases people can experience a complete loss of their own ego identities and feel full identification with the consciousness of some other individual, animal, or even inanimate object.[7]

Investigators interpret such phenomena as the subjects' regression into the history of their own biological and spiritual experience. In psychedelic experiments, quite concrete and realistic situations are often reproduced that are identified as embryonic recollections. It can happen that this regression extends so far that the person experiences episodes not only of his own life but also of the life of his ancestors.

Akin to this type of transpersonal illumination is the discovery of "karmic reality," the experience of past incarnations. Sometimes this can take place in very general form, when people observe the evolution of life in an unending cycle of deaths and new births. In other cases these perceptions are more specific: the subjects see that they themselves existed many times before their present incarnation and that further rebirths await them. At times both these pictures are combined in a single multidimensional perception, and then the subjects may observe the unfolding of their own karmic monad within the framework of much broader cycles of "death and rebirth."[8]

Of course, one is tempted to regard these data as confirming the conception of Samsāra. But another interpretation of transpersonal experience is also possible, one that comes from a particular reconstruction of an archaic perception of the world and the mechanisms whereby information is passed on from generation to generation.

Let us first touch upon some of the distinctive features of archaic perception, bearing in mind, however, that certain difficulties are encountered when making a direct extrapolation of the characteristics of the thought of presently living ethnic groups (at stages of development that in regard to some parameters are near to man's evolution in the early periods of his history) to an understanding of the specific features of the perception and thinking of archaic cultures. We cannot be sure that we will arrive at an appropriate interpretation of the phenomenon of interest to us. It is more appropriate perhaps to speak about revealing a tendency, a certain direction of processes, discernible on the basis of such a comparison. The perception of the world specific to members of some ethnic groups contemporaneous with us should obviously be seen only as a paler copy, a copy of the type of perception characteristic of people of archaic cultures.

The data of contemporary anthropology show that the archaic, "antique" perception was distinguished by its immediacy, its wholeness, and its spontaneity. It was based on a sense of the world characterized by man's being one with the world of nature, man's being immersed in nature, when his own impressions and experiences appeared as a component part, as a continuation of cosmic processes.

The sphere of the psychic contents that formed on the basis of such a perception of the world necessarily had certain specific features. In particular, it was syncretic and holistic, since at the basis of this perception were undifferentiated aggregates of impressions and experiences. Moreover, in this sphere not only was what characterized the state of objective processes not distinguished from what was subjective, but these components themselves—the subjective and the objective—were fused, merged into one. Today we might refer to such a state as a syncretism of the emotional-mental sphere, although this is not quite accurate. In "antique" perception, ideas and emotions not only did not exist separately, they formed mental constructs that differ substantially from contemporary ones (in a certain sense, "protothoughts" and "protoemotions") and that the tools of modern language are hardly sufficient to describe adequately.

Hence we shall resort to illustration as a way of giving an indirect clarification of what we have in mind. Investigators studying so-called "primitive cultures" call attention to the extraordinary acuity, vividness, and supernatural keenness of the way representatives of these cultures typically perceive their environment. Bushmen, for example, are capable of sensing the approach of a person or animal or the onset of some event long before this is possible for a representative of "technocratic civilization."

The basis for this recognition in all probability is an astonishingly thorough assimilation (and even a fusion, an identification) of their own ego with the existence of another—be it human or animal. There are descriptions of how one bushman learned and informed the children of the approach of his father after sensing in his own body the pain from his father's old wounds; or learned that his wife was returning from a neighboring village by having felt on his shoulders the stretched straps with which she held her child on her back. A sensation of wiry hair "growing" on his ribs tells the bushman that an antelope is near, and so forth.

Such a perception (but only more pronounced) of the surrounding world and one's place in it was probably also characteristic of the early stages of evolution of man: the senses were maximally sharpened; inner sensations encompassed not only one's own world but also the world of others, as it were. A man was open to the world as a kind of "sensor" devoid of natural boundaries: the sensation of the fur of an antelope or the rustling of its feet in the dry grass was as much a reality for him as his own world.

Of course, the nature of such a phenomenon, the prerequisites for such complete empathy, such "getting into" the world of another, require study. How is such an identification of oneself with another at all possible? A.I. Kuprin's Olesia, who caused the master to trip and fall on level ground, also got into his image and copied his motions, imagining a string stretched across his path in the process. However, in this case the devices of identification were used consciously. For the bushman, such sensations seem to occur spontaneously.

The comparable capacity for reincarnation, of course, cannot be explained simply in terms of identification of oneself with another. The question is how and why such an identification is possible and through what means is it accomplished. It is also important why these antique forms of perception have been preserved in the present, forms so radically different from those that are usual in contemporary technocratic culture that it is difficult to believe in them and even more difficult to explain them.

It appears that a study of the mechanisms of information transfer from generation to generation can shed some light on these questions. One interesting direction in this area is, for example, the theory of geno-cultural co-evolution, which is a continuation of the above-mentioned sociobiological program.[9] However, in addition to the genetic channel for relaying the experience, other mechanisms for its transmission must also exist, since acquired features, as we know, cannot be inherited. Hence, one must assume that the evolution of human culture is a genetically programmed tendency to augment the adaptive capabilities of the species, which is realized in the form of the retention of the positive and negative experience that is unconditionally significant for survival but cannot be transmitted genetically since it concerns acquired properties, skills, habits, and so forth.

Within the framework of this conception, we should like to discuss a very peculiar mechanism for relaying human experience. Some of its features relate it to genetic evolution, but others are similar to the qualities of cultural evolution: as in genetic evolution, information is transmitted mainly within the framework of consanguineous bonds, from parents to children; but as in cultural evolution, acquired attributes also can be passed on. It is also important that the existence of such a mechanism makes it possible to reveal some nontrivial aspects in our understanding of the nature of transpersonal experience.

The model presented by Eric Berne, the well-known American theoretician of psychoanalysis, offers some good opportunities for discussing this mechanism. In this model, it is assumed that three personalities are contained in every individual: Parent, Adult, and Child. The term 'Parent' signifies ego states similar to those of parental figures. The term 'Adult' refers to ego states that are autonomously elaborated by the individual for an objective appraisal of reality. Finally, the term 'Child' refers to ego states that continue to operate from the moment they are fixated in early childhood and are, to use Berne's expression, archaic relics.[10]

In the context of this conception, the assertion "That is your Parent" means that now you are "in the same state of mind as one of your parents (or a parental substitute) used to be, and you are responding as he would, with the same posture, gestures, vocabulary, feelings, etc." The words "That is your Adult" mean "You have just made an autonomous, objective, appraisal of the situation and are now stating these thought processes, or the problems you perceive, or the conclusions you have come to, in a non-prejudicial manner." The expression "That is your Child" means "The manner and intent of your reaction is the same as it would have been when you were a very little boy or girl."[11]

Although it was elaborated for the analysis of behavioral acts, this conception is of some interest, we think, for interpreting the phenomena of consciousness outlined above. To show this, let us look in a little more detail at the sphere of mental contents designated as "Parent" in the structure of the personality. Through them, the system of the subject's personal meanings is enriched by stereotypes of behavior, of reaction, of reasoning, and so forth that are acquired, not found independently.

As for the person who in his time raised the individual whose personality structure we are analyzing in this particular case and who handed down to the individual his vision of the world, his ways and means of perceiving and interpreting reality, this person in turn also bore within him "Child," "Parent," and "Adult." The content of his "Parent" consisted of stereotypes and habits "handed down gratuitously" to him by the people who raised him. And they in turn bore their "Parents" within them ... Thus the continuity of life experience is preserved even between those generations whose mutual bonds seem to be totally destroyed: the past is forgotten and expunged from people's memory. But let us not be hasty with our conclusions. Through the action of this unique mechanism of transference, all the changes in social consciousness associated with the history and culture of the people to which the given individual belongs are "built into" the structure of his personality, and largely independently of his will and his wishes. This historical and cultural experience predetermines many forms of a person's life activity, as well as the variants of his individual reactions to events taking place around him, their evaluation, and so forth.

As applied to the problem with which we are presently concerned, this is all important insofar as such long sequences of mediations make it possible for the individual to gain access to ways of receiving and representing information that existed in the distant past and are nontypical for contemporary culture (and, it should be mentioned in passing, that serve, among other things, as a source of creative decisions, nontrivial associations, analogies, and judgments). These ways and means of perceiving and interpreting the world that are alternatives in relation to our civilization not only are not lost as the early stages of the evolution of thinking recede into the past but continue to function, constituting an inseparable part of every individual's thinking capacity. They "supply" him with a mental content formed as a result of his assimilation of the reality characteristic of his times and his culture but using mechanisms of perception and information processing that turn out to be inherited from his primogenitors.

What can this approach provide for a rational interpretation of transpersonal experience? As already pointed out, experimental studies have shown that man has the capacity to recollect and reproduce remote events of childhood, which he could not know from others but whose reliability was confirmed by any of the persons around him at the time. This capacity for reproduction seems astonishing but not excessively so. It fits in principle into the existing model of memory, according to which memory is thought to retain all events happening to a person throughout his lifetime. It is simply that access to the various domains of memory is so difficult that reproduction is possible only under special conditions (hypnosis, the effect of psychedelics, or, for example, electrical stimulation of certain areas of the brain). As a result, pictures of days far off in the past and never reproduced suddenly surge into our memory, and, what is more, they are accompanied by the entire wealth of sensations and experiences that accompanied the person's state at that time.

Things more difficult to interpret begin when an individual, in moving along the path of the inner experiences of his altered consciousness, suddenly begins to recollect what happened when he was in his mother's womb and, further, what happened "when he was not a person." Here, strictly speaking, begins what is the most difficult to explain. When representatives of contemporary culture encounter such information, the most common reaction is to reject it as unscientific, as charlatanism, as something that cannot be. This reaction is entirely natural and understandable. It has an adaptive, protective function and is aimed at avoiding a direct clash between the person and facts that, if he accepted them, would confront him with serious internal problems. After all, we know that as the personality develops it gives rise to intellectual structures in which are registered the traditions of the given community and the elements of scientific knowledge, established mental stereotypes, and so forth that are dispersed within it. A considerable share of this "baggage" of knowledge and ideas is assimilated by the subject uncritically and unconsciously, simply as a consequence of his life activity in growing up. Such intellectual structures can sometimes be placed in doubt by circumventing the barriers to critical thought, but, once they are accepted, they still preserve considerable powers of resistance against potential counterexamples.

On the contrary, beliefs and notions that passed the checkpoints of consciousness at least once can be checked again. True, the deeper they have "grown" into the individual system of personal meanings and the more bonds, dependencies, and relations are based on these premises, the more difficult it is to cast doubt upon them. This is one of the reasons why it is not so easy to overcome stereotypes and why a truly creative step, the rejection of established initial limitations in interpreting anything at all, requires of a person special personal qualities, including the courage to put himself on the block and lower his defenses against his surroundings. To form a new "frame" of ideas that organize the world in a different way requires time, sometimes quite a bit of time. Throughout all this time, a person remains quite unprotected from the standpoint of his capacity for effective adaptation. (Some investigators, by the way, see in this one of the reasons for the crisis periods in individual development.)

However, the situation becomes even more dramatic if the sphere of personal meanings is touched, since this sphere is populated by things that did not pass the critical threshold in their time. These are even deeper, more archaic layers of the human psyche, which form the very foundation of a person's system for perceiving the world and understanding his place in it. They are all the more stable since they are practically never placed in doubt. It is for this reason that they represent the most reliable link (or one of the most reliable links) among all those serving as the foundation of a person's system for interpreting the world.

All in all, this is a very intelligent mechanism. It is just such components of the system of personal meanings that, serving as the foundation of this system, will become least susceptible to "counterexamples" and will maximize the stability of the overall system of a person's knowledge and notions. This means that they will be the best at fulfilling one of the most important functions of all—ensuring the subject's effective adaptation to the constantly changing conditions of his environment.

A reliable guarantee that such a choice will be made is the circumstance that many generations of people have lived basing their individual systems for viewing the world on these unshakeable and unconscious postulates. Real parents make sure that this experience is passed on to their children. The inner "Parents" in each of us attentively and solicitously see to it that the prohibitions, taboos, indisputable truths, and so forth that exist in society are never placed in doubt by our inner "Adult" or "Child."

Thus the spontaneous reaction of rejecting information at variance with some quite stable stereotypes is a thoroughly natural consequence of the triggering of mechanisms that ensure the safekeeping and stable functioning of the subject's inner self.

But now, taking into account what we have said, let us consider how it is possible for a person to "recollect" what happened before he was born. The most likely answer may be that the characteristics of the archaic perception of the world of which we spoke earlier are not lost as man moves further away from his ancestors, who lived in the early stages of evolution, but are forever "built into" (through language, through habits and traditions, through systems of stereotypes and beliefs) his subconscious. The mechanism for passing on cultural-historical experience through the system of "Child–Parent" relations in turn ensures that this specific perception of the world (as well as the information that has been and will be received on its basis) is passed on to each subsequent generation. (The degree of accessibility of such information and the degree of mastery of the corresponding capabilities by representatives of the contemporary technocratic culture are another matter. In our view, it is higher among members of traditional communities, who have retained quite "solid" ethnic structures.)

The aggregate action of these two factors—the specific nature of an archaic perception of the world and the possibility of passing on its basic structures to each subsequent generation through a mechanism for handing down vitally significant cultural information—is the basis that enables us to explain roughly how a person can "recollect" something that happened before his birth.

If at earlier stages of evolution the perception of the world was such that the subject was fully open to perceptions from without, was as if dissolved in his surroundings and the surroundings seemed to be part of him, then, probably, it really is possible to acquire such specific knowledge[12] as the consequence of a profound empathetic identification of a person with the world of other people, animals, and natural phenomena. It seems to us that one can understand on this basis, without resorting to mystical models and without denying the manifest possibility that such perceptual phenomena so untypical of our culture can exist (phenomena that are the stuff of trans-personal experience), why modern man, by immersing himself in the past, is capable of feeling himself to be an animal, a bird, a tree, or some other person.[13]

Thus all these data can be interpreted as evidencing not that man at one time or other was this or that creature but indeed something quite different. They can mean that the human memory retains not only components of a person's own experience acquired in the process of his life activity and not only some stock of impersonal general cultural information. There is hidden in it also a long sequence of personal incarnations of this culture that links the present with the initial stages of human evolution. In any event, the character of the forms of consciousness we have examined in the foregoing corresponds with that level of man's phylogenetic evolution in which his perception enabled him fully to fuse and dissolve himself in his surroundings and identify himself with another and feel that other as a component part of his own self. At that stage, experience that today is reproduced in sessions using psychedelics, hallucinogens, and other means for influencing the consciousness in order to study its transformations was accessible to man, it seems, without his having to undergo any real transformations.

Notes

1. See W.R. Trevathan, *Human Birth: An Evolutionary Perspective* (New York: Aldine de Gruyter, 1987).
2. See F.B. Berezin, "Nekotorye mekhanizmy intrapsikhologicheskoi adaptatsii i psikhosomaticheskie sootnosheniia," in *Bessoznatel'noe* (Tbilisi, 1978), vol. 2, pp. 285–87.
3. See E.O. Wilson, *On Human Nature* (Cambridge, MA: Harvard University Press, 1978), pp. 175–77.
4. *Tibetskaia "Kniga mertvykh" (Bardo Tedol)* (Moscow, 1992).
5. 'Bardo' is an intermediate state: 'Bar' means 'between' and 'do' means 'two.'
6. *Tibetskaia "Kniga mertvykh"*, pp. 19–28.
7. S. Grof and J. Halifax, *The Human Encounter with Death* (London, 1978), pp. 54–55.
8. Ibid., pp. 58–59.
9. See, for example, J. Lamsden and A. Gushurst, "Gene–Culture Coevolution: Humankind to the Moving," in *Sociobiology and Epistemology*, Synthese Library, vol. 180 (Dordrecht, 1985), pp. 3–31.
10. E. Berne, *Games People Play: The Psychology of Human Relationships* (New York: Grove Press, 1964), p. 23.
11. Ibid., p. 24.
12. Although, of course, this is not knowledge in the modern sense of the word but the subject's state of mind of another modality, which it is difficult to find an analog to in our language and our culture. It is something like confidence, in which the component of doubt is not simply absent but impossible.
13. Moreover, it turns out that he very correctly reproduces many distinctive features of the life activity of those beings in whom he is "reincarnated" in the course of the

session (including, for example, the psychology of animals about which he did not even have an idea in a normal state of consciousness). What is more, in reproducing episodes from the life of his ancestors, the subject describes details extremely accurately—the clothing of past epochs, the architecture, weapons, ritual practices, and so forth.

B.I. PRUZHININ

Astrology

Science, Pseudoscience, Ideology?

A half century of intensive educational propaganda has finally had its fitting effect: astrological notions are being assimilated these days in our country with striking ease and moreover above all by educated, so to speak enlightened, people. It has become good tone to listen on every occasion to the forecasts of fashionable astrologers, to interview them, and to print computer horoscopes. The traditional skepticism of our scientists barely suffices them to keep their own scientific view of the world intact. But if any understanding is to be achieved about the phenomenon of the present-day astrological renaissance, it can only be done in connection with science. For over two thousand years, astrology has endeavored to become a respectable science, and for this reason alone, any analytical approach to astrological material must, in any event initially, regard this material as scientific.

On the sources of astrology

In their prognostications, serious astrologers have always noted the rationality of astrology's methods, the accuracy of its calculations, and the rigor of its arguments. And indeed, astrology has reached a quite high level of rationalization in its notions of the dependencies that exist (of course, from its standpoint) between "earthly" events, that is, events happening here on Earth, to us or around us, and "celestial" events, happening there, in the Heavens, to the various heavenly bodies. It is this rationalization that distinguishes astrology from all other forms of divinatory practices, including astral divination.

Russian text © 1994 by the Presidium of the Russian Academy of Sciences. "Astrologiia: nauka, psevdonauka, ideologiia?" *Voprosy filosofii*, 1994, no. 2, pp. 13–24. A publication of the Institute of Philosophy, Russian Academy of Sciences.

Boris Isaevich Pruzhinin is a Doctor of Philosophical Sciences and executive secretary of the editorial board of *Voprosy filosofii*.

Predictions based on the stars can be made even without rationalizing conceptions about the connection existing between "given" and "celestial" events. One can predict from the stars fully disregarding astrological theory or without even suspecting it exists. However, such a practice belongs to another type of cultural activity, where there is place, say, for various kinds of "-mancies" but no place for "-logies." The profound typological differences between these kinds of cultural activity are certainly not effaced by the fact that there is a clear continuity and affinity among the common ideas on which they are based. Astrology is a recent acquisition of mankind; it emerged roughly at the same time as the whole of European science. Astral divination is at least twice as old. Evidence that people revered and worshipped the stars comes to us from the deepest antiquity.

Life itself, the everyday life of hunters, shepherds, and later farmers, engendered the idea that there was some sort of dependence of earthly events on the position and movement of the stars. The stars really did play a tremendous role in this life, one that we today find difficult to imagine. The rhythms of the starry heavens set practically all the vital and technological cycles of ancient man. People found their place in space and time by the stars. The diurnal cycles of the Sun and the Moon and the seasonal changes in the starry heavens served as a natural yardstick, which people used to begin, synchronize, and carry to completion everything they did. Let us state from the outset: no matter how naively the ancients interpreted the nature of the interference of the stars in earthly matters, the objective fact itself of such interference cannot elicit any doubt. People in fact set the rhythms of their everyday lives and their technologies by the stars, and this real rhythmization formed a basic core around which their equally real experience was concentrated. The cultural forms for consolidating this experience could be the most varied, including even ritual dances and mystical rituals, but the experience itself was as real, uncontrived, and nonillusory as the astrally set rhythm of people's everyday life was uncontrived and nonillusory. Later this experience in fact formed the foundation of effective divinatory predictions and then of astrological calculations. However, the latter required special conditions, for in itself such experience was neither rational nor, all the more so, scientific.

The transition from practical life experience to scientific experience and, accordingly, from divination to scientifically grounded prediction (which astrology claims for itself) requires as a minimum a conscious cultural orientation toward a rational selection of and perfection of the methods of prediction. In everyday practical life, few people are concerned, say, with the task of consciously creating situations in which the circumstances of some prediction would be deliberately varied in order to ascertain the range of validity of that prediction. In science, tasks of this sort are the norm of everyday work. A cultural orientation conducive to scientific activity established itself, as we know, only in Greece in the fifth century B.C. And at roughly the same time, astrology as well was born within the context of the formation of a universally recognized science.

True, one peculiar feature was discernible in the development of astrology from the very outset. Its scientific status was formed above all through its assimilation of external forms for rationally recording and organizing experience, forms that genuinely admitted the improvement of predictive practices. But astrology never showed any notable enthusiasm at all as regards the cultural orientation whose realization in practice constituted in fact the phenomenon of rational science.

The application of the language of mathematics (mainly the language of geometry) to the techniques of astral divination made for its formal rationalization and opened up the possibility of unifying, rigorously organizing, and rendering examinable the vast mass of varied and diverse experience accumulated over millennia. All this became possible in full measure with the appearance of rational astronomical models of celestial dynamics (Eudoxus of Cnidus, about 406 to about 355 B.C.). Astral divination based on precise, highly rationalized notions of the structure of the astral heavens and accomplished using mathematical models earned the proud title of a "-logy." After all, a rationalization of this sort really did open the way to the possibility of clarifying scientifically the idea that terrestrial and celestial events were linked, of taking into account the most subtle nuances of this link and, accordingly, of continuously improving the central idea of astrology as mathematics and astronomy themselves were improved, and, what is especially important, of controlling the accuracy of astrological predictions. How astrology made use of this capability is another question. But in one way or other, the application of the precise language of astronomy and mathematics to the technique of astral divination transformed this technique into an intellectual structure that was in many respects similar to science. In ancient Rome, in any event, astrologers were simply called mathematicians, and mathematics at that time was one of the synonyms for science.

On the structure of astrological knowledge

The term 'astrology' is used to designate both astrological theory and practical astrology, that is, the activity of crafting astrological prognostications for specific people or communities. As a rule it is in sciences of the social and humanistic sort that such a combination occurs. Astrology could be ranked among them as well, although heavenly bodies are directly in the center of its attention. The astrologer sees "terrestrial," human meanings in the movement of the "stars."

Astrological theory contains quite an abundant mass of accurate and objective information about the heavenly bodies, the character of their movement, their trajectories, and their relative positions. This information is certainly not the exclusive property of astrology, but until comparatively recently it was astrology that was often the basic agent of its elaboration. Thus, almost to the end of the nineteenth century, it was astrologers who published regularly updated tables and calendars (the ephemerides) indicating all the possible movements of the heavenly bodies for each year, thereby enriching the store of general astronomical knowledge. But this information also has certain peculiarities.

It should above all be noted that the astronomical-astrological stage on which the stellar analog of earthly events and destinies unfolds has a geocentric design. After Copernicus, this position was defended by the argument that it was Man and, accordingly, man's habitat, Earth, that was at the center of the astrological cosmos. Astrology is not at all interested in the whole starry sky. The planets of the solar system (and in astrology it is they that are the most active and dynamic factors of influence) move over the sky in roughly the same plane. Hence the astrological cosmos is a gigantic disc ("wheel"), at the center of which is Earth, and the external vault is formed by a quite narrow strip of the heavens with slowly moving constellations against the background of which the planets move relatively rapidly. The constellations on this strip of the heavens are in fact the well-known twelve constellations of the Zodiac.[1]

The planets of the solar system (as they are seen from Earth) form complex and constantly changing figures against the background of the Zodiac constellations (in one of which the sun is to be found at a given time). The aggregate action of these planets, intermeshed with the action of the Zodiac stellar background, in fact determines the possible paths on which terrestrial situations may unfold. The proper task of astrology is to define accurately and rigorously the overall character (quality) and overall intensity (quantity) of this aggregate action. This is done by evaluating the intensity and significance of each factor acting separately and of their reciprocal actions. One can, of course, doubt the arguments of astrologers concerning the nature and character of the influence of stars on earthly matters, but there is nothing supernatural or antiscientific to be found here.

When some planet is observed in a part of the heavens occupied by some specific constellation, an astrologer says[2] that the planet is in that constellation. The point is that radiation coming from this constellation and this planet are parallel, and consequently, their influences combine. Accordingly, if we say that Mars is in Aries, this means that an observer on Earth looking at the sky will find the planet Mars among the stars forming the constellation we know as the constellation of Aries; and since the influence of Aries resonates with the influence that expresses the strongest side of Mars's nature, we evaluate Mars in this case as "exalted" [in older terminology, "dignified"—Ed.]. An astrologer can then calculate these influences with the aid of a quite complex mathematical apparatus.

A mathematical model of the heavens is another extremely important component of astrological theory. The circle of the Zodiac is graduated (360˚); then it is divided into twelve equal parts of 30˚ each (which in general corresponds to the twelve constellations of the Zodiac); each part in turn is divided into three parts (decants), and so forth. The resultant model of the Heavens makes it possible to determine quantitatively spheres of influence and the direction and the limits of the action and interaction of the heavenly bodies. Astrology projects the effective dynamics of the heavenly bodies (as seen from Earth!) onto this formal picture, constructed according to rigorous rules. The rhythms of the Universe become calculable: the astrologer is able to calculate the future course of celestial events and their relation to earthly events and hence to compute earthly events. The formalized model of the Starry Heavens with its rigorously graduated orbits and mathematically defined topology, with its strict measurement of influences, renders the Word of the Universe, which also articulates our earthly being, intelligible. But to understand the meaning of what has been said, the meanings of the words uttered must also still be understood!

The dynamics of the starry heavens interests astrologers insofar as it says something about earthly matters. Astrology is not a science about the stars but a science about people. What, for example, does it mean that Mars moves from the constellation of Aries into the constellation of Taurus or that from the standpoint of an earthly observer Mars forms an angle of 30˚ with Venus? What does this mean not for the heavenly body named Mars but for us, for those to whom the astrologer intends to communicate something important, that is, something directly concerning us, as he reads the Book of the Heavens? This level of astrological knowledge (the third component of theoretical astrology) is presented in the form of a series of special hypotheses, which, in the terminology of contemporary methodology of science, may be called metalinguistic or inter-pretive:

"Mars is a soldier. Courageous, energetic, stern, ferocious, cruel, full of aspirations, although perhaps not especially intelligent. He easily loses control of himself, he is quick in word and deed . . ."

It is these hypotheses that define the initial subject of astrology, while astronomical information and the mathematical apparatus serve only to add precision to them. And, moreover, it is these hypotheses that must be subjected to a rationally organized empirical verification in the science of astrology, for they are in fact the hypotheses about the nature and character of the astrological connection between earthly and heavenly events. The various mathematical and astronomical structures serve only to define them more precisely. Let me give an example. For an observer to be able to record the position in the heavenly vault of any two planets from Earth, he obviously must change the orientation of his telescope, shifting it from planet to planet. The angles thus formed are the famous "aspects of the planets." Thus some of these angles mark the qualitative results of the interaction of these planets in a rigorously quantitative way. Let us say a trigon (an angle of 120°), a sextile (60°), and a semi-sextile reinforce the corresponding favorable influence of the interacting planets on Earth, while a quartile (or quadrate—90°) imparts an ill-fated character to their action. Accordingly, in astrology we can in principle establish quite accurately what earthly meaning the action of any partic-ular planet has in a corresponding environment. However, neither accu-rate measurements of the positions of the planets nor rigorous mathematical calculations of their interrelations clarify the conditions for the realization of the strictly meaningful aspect of their influence on earthly affairs.

That slightly reddish little star we can see with the naked eye on a clear night—why is it masculine? What are the features that identify its gender? And where do we get the idea that Mars is malicious and aggres-sive? From the standpoint of standard scientific methodology, we would have to answer these questions, for example, as follows: these notions arose, in particular, because Mars in fact "protects" soldiers, hangmen, and doctors (i.e., people whose profession in one way or another involves bloodshed), which is expressed in such-and-such rigorously recordable and quantitatively expressible events, actions, and dependencies. Then should follow an analysis of cases in which the protection of Mars is expressed in one way or other. However, astrologers have in essence never engaged in such work and, moreover, as we shall attempt to show below, for quite fundamental reasons.

Do astrological hypotheses have any foundation?

As we know, interpretation is an intellectual procedure whereby a system of signs, formally organized but signifying nothing (in this case, the system of heavenly bodies in relation to earthly events), is ascribed (earthly) meanings such that the formal system becomes a contentful, meaningful language that tells us something about our earthly matters. So, then, on closer examination, we find that the basic interpretive hypotheses of astrology do not raise its formal system to a level permitting any objective verification of the sort associated with exact natural science. The metalanguage of astrology is rich and varied, but it is based on hypotheses that ascribe to objective heavenly processes purely subjective meanings, that is, meanings that relate to man's subjective world. These hypotheses are used to interpret the spatial position, mutual location, and dynamics of the heavenly bodies in terms of personal life situations and human interrelations. But this is a very special reality, requiring a specific relationship toward it and not amenable to simple verification for reproducibility or especially to experiments. True, there is a thoroughly material aspect to this reality—if, let us say, the evaluations of "happy" or "unhappy" are obviously relative and can change places literally before our eyes, then such events as marriage, the birth of a child, its gender, death, and so forth can, of course, be established quite definitely. But, since such events are woven into the fabric of life, where the meaning side is still the determining aspect, even such obvious circumstances of human existence as birth and death take on an ambiguity and conditionality. And astrology in its interpretive structures has always been oriented primarily to the personally meaningful subtext of human interrelations.

The planet Mars appears as the bearer of the active, militarist male principle in astrological hypotheses. That is the essence of its influence on earthly affairs. However, Mars's aggressiveness can be moderated somewhat if the feminine Venus is situated at a strictly defined angle (aspect) relative to Mars and if, moreover, Mars is ascending into the constellation of soothing Pisces; but if Mars during the period of its ascendancy is in the constellation of the aggressor Leo or in its own "house," in the constellation of the butting Aries, and, moreover, in its own month, in March, then its proper influence will be especially active and it will be especially intensively protective of, as we have said, soldiers, hangmen, doctors, and cooks. Mars is a male planet, the moon and Venus are female planets, while Mercury (Hermes) is a hermaphrodite and, according to the ancient astrological tradition, behaves like a man among male planets and like a woman among female planets (although today the diametrically opposite logic of behavior would seem more plausible). And so on. Such interpretive hypotheses of the respective evolutions of the heavenly bodies appear as analogs to the unfolding of the life situations in which specific people, groups of people, states, and nations operate. The same structure of interpersonal relations may be projected onto one's state of mind, onto the state of one's health, or onto a commercial enterprise. This structure is in general universal and in principle permits celestial evolutions to be brought into correlation with any human affairs whatsoever, provided only that these affairs can always be represented in terms of human relations. But what these hypotheses totally lack is precision and definitiveness, so necessary for scientific hypotheses, in regard to the conditions of their realization. No mathematical calculations can render anything about the action of stars more precise insofar as it concerns the experience of grief or joy, the sense of success or failure . . . The arguments of astrologers are always too indefinite to incorporate them into a standard experimental situation.

However, they are definite enough for them to be understood by a person who is even only superficially conversant with the corresponding tradition. And not only to be understood but also to be adopted as guidelines for his activity.

We are not now and obviously will never be able to demonstrate experimentally and empirically the truthfulness or falsehood of the interpretive hypotheses of astrology. But, in addition to scientific argumentation based on reason, there is another type of argument, perhaps even stronger and in any case more widespread: there is also argument from tradition. In antiquity, the planet Mars was dedicated to war, and the Babylonians associated this planet with the god of death, Ninib. . . . Obviously something quite serious is behind these beliefs of the ancients—some sort of thousand-year experience. And science, incidentally, draws rather actively on this experience. It is, by the way, not at all interested in where this or that idea comes from or what is the source for the emergence of scientific hypotheses in our heads (on this plane science is very similar to poetry). Thus scientific ideas can be borrowed from traditional beliefs as well—the most important thing is that there is some real content behind these ideas. However, for science as well as for poetry, their own way of representing ideas is important. Scientific ideas must be grounded in a thoroughly specific, polished, scientifically accepted method; any deviations from the standards of scientific argument places that particular intellectual structure outside science.

In the astronomical part of astrology, every judgment is in one way or another based on observations of the stars and on theories constructed on these observations. An astrologer usually argues in conformity with the standards of science (although his arguments are by no means always incontestable). The mathematical models of astrology are based on other foundations that do not require a direct appeal to an empirical experience. But the rational grounds of mathematics are no less serious a foundation for scientific argument than are direct observations and experiments. However, when it comes to earthly interpretations of heavenly events of practical relevance for life, in astrology they are neither directly nor indirectly based on either rational arguments or empirical or logical substantiation, and hence they cannot be called scientific under any circumstances.

Aleister Crowley, quoted above, a very notable twentieth-century figure in astrology who has done much to restore its former grandeur in our enlightened age, dealt with this problem as follows:

> Those who are familiar with Greek and Roman mythology are able to extract from this circumstance very important information about the meanings of the planets. To do this, one need only concentrate one's attention on the attributes of the gods whose names have been given to the respective planets. Indeed, in general there simply is no better method for studying this matter; for the names were ascribed to the planets by no means accidentally. It was done on the basis of a careful examination of their astrological influences.[3]

If one leaves out of account the last sentence, in which an attempt is made to shift onto the ancients the work of providing a scientific grounding for astrological interpretations, everything here is quite obvious. In its central point, astrology gives us neither an empirical foundation (observation, experiment, the search for counterexamples, etc.) nor theoretical arguments (evaluation of theoretical constructs for their thoroughness and non-contradictoriness, correspondence of astrological theories with one another and with the theoretical constructs of other sciences and the scientific picture of the world as a whole); astrology offers us an argument from Tradition.

Nowadays much is said about the relativity of the standards of science, of their sociocultural dependence, and, accordingly, of the sociocultural dependence of science itself. Some leaders of the postpositivist wave in methodology, especially Paul Feyerband, have done much to promote views according to which science can be distinguished neither from constructs that have the appearance of being scientific nor even from myth. Indeed, it cannot be denied that a science oriented toward unchanging standards is doomed to stagnation and that in real science there is very much that is relative to cultural-historical, social, and even personal circumstances. Nonetheless, there is science and there is nonscience: no science, even the most rational, can avoid appealing to tradition, but it is certainly not tradition that defines the profile of science.

Tradition and reason in astrology

Let me stress once again—the mere fact of orientation toward tradition, toward experience handed down by tradition from generation to generation, by no means discredits this experience. A great deal of what we learn comes not at all from scientific conceptions, and we are far from accepting it on the strength of rational grounding. There are cultural contents that by no means fit into rational forms. But there are also cultural functions that only reason is capable of fulfilling. For example, only reason is capable of shaping objective knowledge about the world, that is, of forming models that can be evaluated as true or false upon being correlated with reality and that are accepted or rejected on the basis of just this parameter. Tradition has its own parameters for evaluation, its own cultural functions, and its own forms for establishing adequacy to the world.

Tradition is linked in the most direct manner with human connections, with processes unfolding on the basis of human interrelations, and hence is always colored in some kind of emotional subjective tones. Strictly speaking, being part of or not being part of human interrelations is what signifies that a tradition is accepted or rejected. A tradition, incidentally, does not disappear when people argue against it, try to eradicate it, or prohibit it, thereby introducing the pathos of rejection into the struggle against it—a tradition may flourish quite well thanks to the efforts of its opponents. A tradition dies when it finds no place for itself in people's lives, when people simply lose interest in it. A living tradition must necessarily be part of people's live, everyday perception of the world. And it achieves this thanks to its extreme flexibility, thanks to the fact that it accepts the presence of mutually contradictory but also mutually complementary positions in its experience, so that we are able to incorporate one or another proposition into our activity depending on the place and the situation. That is why traditional "popular wisdom," let us say, is so alive when it says on one occasion that "boldness conquers cities" and on other occasions "the more quietly you go, the further you will get." The techniques of all "-mancies," divinations, and predictions of clairvoyants are based on this same ambiguity of the argument from tradition. All of these require coparticipation of the "object" of divination, which, being itself involved emotionally in the process of predicting its own (the "object's") future, thus concretizes the experience of the tradition on which the diviner relies. Astrology concretizes its interpretive hypotheses in a similar manner.

According to ancient tradition, Mars in opposition to Saturn brings happiness to a ruler, while in opposition to Jupiter it brings ruin to the country. But both the ruler and the country are given a chance to figure out themselves what in the particular situation is happiness and what is ruin for them.

In ordinary, so to speak everyday, nonprofessional divination, such a technique of ambiguity often becomes a self-sufficient means of prediction. But thereby for all practical purposes it severs its links to real experience as concretized in tradition. Thus the technique of reading fortunes from cards now usually relies solely on the perspicuity and personal experience of the diviner, for there is no longer any tradition behind the infinitely foggy semantics of contemporary playing cards; on the other hand, the "object" of divination becomes a full-fledged coparticipant here and in the course of a thoroughly emotional association with the diviner decides for himself what is and how long should be the "long road" and what sort of an institution the "official building" is. Sometimes, astrology descends to the same level; most mass printings of horoscopes are precisely like this if only because they disregard the planetary deployment particular to every individual. I, however, will regard such a situation of a break with tradition as a degenerate case and not a case typical for astrology, despite the fact that it is extremely prevalent.

Present-day astrology endeavors to remain true to the content of tradition (i.e., the real experience of organizing life in accordance with the stars that tradition hands down). Hence the degree of ambiguity of astrological claims is moderated. This is happening, in particular, for the simple reason that astrology managed nonetheless to work out its own written language, and astrologers are engaged, albeit sporadically, in the historical-critical elaboration of their conceptual and formal-mathematical apparatus, giving it access to the real experience of tradition.

Of course, there is always the danger here that astrology will be transformed into a natural science, which would also signify a break with tradition. But astrology has a very rich experience in balancing different forms of reduction and has devised, it must be said, a very effective system of means for such balancing. Astrology has always seen its immediate objective to be not reflecting reality "as it is" or explaining the world but rather influencing the fates of unique "objects" (the fates of individual people or communities). Hence, when astrologers discuss and evaluate astrological texts, their task is not so much analytical as practical—improving the paradigm of successful astrological activity, that is, perfecting the means for successful partaking of the content of tradition. This success is achieved not at all by a rational clarification of the conditions of astrological prediction (it is difficult even to imagine what the "resolution" of the conceptual apparatus and the measuring procedure must be in order to calculate the trajectory of a particular human destiny!). This success is achieved precisely by virtue of the "fogginess" and ambiguity of rational (including mathematical) astrological arguments, which enable astrology to make the client a coparticipant in his own predictions. In addition, partaking of tradition is preserved in astrology also because it does not restrict itself merely to giving the "object" of its prediction a chance to make conjectures about its unclear and ambiguous places but in fact shifts his participation to the practical plane. Astrology gives the "object" of prediction the chance to become a "subject," the chance to make a real free choice, that is, the chance to act in reality, taking into account the Word of the Stars. Thus the "object" of astrological prediction enters into dialogue with the Stars rather than remaining a passive listener and executor of the Will of the Heavens. The idea of a rigorous unequivocal correspondence between events on Earth and events in the Heavens, on which all astrological computations are based—the "theory of natal signs" [*teoriia genitur*]—is complemented in astrology by a theory that essentially excludes this idea—the "theory of initiatives" [i.e., by "elective astrology."—Ed.]

More on the sources of astrology

Astrologers themselves turn above all to ancient Babylon in seeking the sources of their science. It was there that the intellectual foundations of astrology were laid, not least because the Babylonians did not stress the divine nature of the stars that circled the heavenly vault in an orderly way and with regularity. It was this orderliness that undercut the idea of their divine sovereignty. An incontestably divine nature was ascribed only to those heavenly bodies that by their deviation from movement in accordance with strict rules demonstrated that a completely self-sufficient force lived in them. The planets behave in this way in our firmament. And once attention was shifted from rhythmically repeating signs (in reference to which plowing, harvesting, the flooding of rivers, and maximum sexual activity began) to arrhythmic signs, the way was open to the possibility of predicting events that were not obligatory but unique, such as victory or defeat in war and the fates of kingdoms and kings.

The answers to such questions were expected primarily from the seven "planets" (in quotes because the Sun was included among them). And the heavens began to speak: the heavenly bodies appeared as a unique alphabet, the letters of which, arranging themselves in different order and in different sequences, formed words, and the play of their multidimensional combinations displayed before the attentive reader a complex text unique in its content. This text was always incomplete, not fully expressed, admitting corrections and the emergence of new meanings; it was a text in which man himself, his sights set on the future, waiting for events and striving either to bring these events closer or to avoid them, had a hand in creation, together with the Heavens. The "theory of initiatives" is a doctrine of how, by means of astrology, to avoid these predicted events—that is, events that strictly speaking are predetermined by the stars.

The Stoics, incidentally—perhaps the only ancient school of philosophy supporting astrology—were emphatically against the theory of initiatives: man can acquire knowledge about his own destiny, but this knowledge will enable him only to accept the inevitable courageously. Astrologers, however, by the very nature of the work in which they are occupied, have not been able to accept this logically inevitable thesis. For astrology is possible only if it is oriented toward the coparticipation in a destiny of the "object" of this destiny.

As times changed, so did ideas about the participation of astrology in practical matters. In the Orient in antiquity, those who read the stars assumed that the stars were concerned only with the destinies of kings and kingdoms. In Greece, the stars were democratized. In the hotbed of political passions of imperial Rome, where for understandable reasons interest in the future of political leaders had by no means just a personal meaning, astrologers, obviously not without hints from the authorities, came to the conclusion that the emperor was perhaps alone in not being subject to the influence of the stars. But even so, regardless of the dangers, astrology was always in one way or another oriented to its client and hence always in one way or another allowed him the possibility of acting according to his own will. For only on this condition did astrological information about the stars acquire concrete meaning for people, affect their private interests, and have a practical meaning for them. And no matter how rigorously the central thesis of astrology—the "thesis of universal sympathy" [i.e., the idea of "correspondences"—Ed.]—affirmed that the diverse combinations of the planets, in concentrating their action on an infant being born and thereby leaving an indelible imprint on him, determining his appearance, his character, and his fate, there was nonetheless always room enough in this action of the stars and in the indeterminacy of the moment of birth for a person to have the possibility of participating effectively himself in shaping his own future.

On the cultural status of astrology
(from an epistemological point of view)

The contradiction so clearly expressed in the contrast between the theory of initiatives and the theory of natal signs pervades the whole of astrology. But this is not a flaw in the astrological constructions but, in my view, the very essence of astrology, its constitutive principle. For it is because of this internal duality that astrology acquired the possibility of looking into the supernatural world of human existence with the aid of its not so very complicated computations and not too broad information from the domain of natural science. According to astrology, the stars move according to their own laws, but rhythms that are the same for the whole of the Universe resonate in their movement, rhythms to which human existence is also subject. Neither astronomical nor physical descriptions of the movement of the stars allow such rhythms to be detected so fully; such descriptions embrace only certain general aspects of reality, omitting what is most important for man—the layer of reality where meaning resides. Of course, one can, moving along the path of natural science, clarify our notions about rhythms that are the same for man and for the stars. One can, if one accepts the general idea that there is a connection between earthly and heavenly events, render explicit the content of tradition by observation and experiment so as to reveal recurrent dependencies and reproducible situations. This method is being worked on intensively right now. For example, A.L. Chizhevskii's hypotheses that solar radiation (the rhythms of solar activity) influences the organisms of animals and man has received weighty confirmation (as a result primarily of statistical studies). In addition, man's venture into space spawned a whole set of scientific disciplines in which the ancient idea that stars influence earthly affairs is being taken up in a new way and in a new experimental context.

But all these things are only a single, and moreover the only natural, side of the unity of man and the Universe. A generalization of data relevant to this aspect will indisputably help us clarify and better explain why, for example, in getting behind the wheel of our automobile, we should not ignore reports on peaks of solar activity. But the question of how solar rhythms are refracted in every individual destiny, of what significance a particular situation on the Sun assumes for me personally, remains beyond the framework of such studies. Even statistical dependencies cannot be traced, for there is no single scale of evaluation. Thus, as regards broad massive influences of the "stars" on man, on his organism and psyche, and, accordingly, on the motivation of his deeds, it would be overhasty to deny the significance of stellar rhythms. And astrology, it must be said, takes such influences into account quite sufficiently. But it is not content with the mass effect of their action, for within the bounds of predictions constructed solely on the basis of this kind of knowledge, it is impossible to compute the trajectory of an individual destiny. And the more astrology tries to imitate science in this regard, the less interesting it becomes as astrology.

The experience of conducting one's life by the stars is by no means only the experience of people's physical (objective) existence. It is also the experience of conducting an interpersonal, normative, cultural, meaningful life in which magnetic storms and atmospheric pressure changes, caused also by cosmic rhythms, of course play their role, but certainly not a determining role. It is this experience, the experience of adjusting the rhythm of the meaningful side of life to the rhythms of the Stars, that the astrological tradition strives above all to preserve, for such experience can in general only be handed down by tradition and not by statistical tables or formulas.

A study undertaken relatively recently by the French scholar Michel Gauquelin will help us to clarify the methodological aspect of how tradition is perceived by the "object" of astrological predictions.[4] Gauquelin reconstructed the positions of the "planets" at the time of birth of 576 members of the French Academy of Medicine, and the result was stunning: the star position favorable for physicians considerably exceeded the mean probability of its occurrence. Gauquelin continued his work: the statistical samples grew, and together with Françoise Gauquelin he studied the archival data of 40,000 persons and in general found some quite stable correlations. For example, he found that when Mars was in the ascendant (from ascent to culmination), there was an increase in the frequency of birth of people who later on would become natural scientists, doctors, athletes, military men, and businessmen. But the average frequency of professions in the sample gave a different distribution: politicians, actors, and journalists and rarely writers, artists, and musicians. And if Jupiter was in the ascendant, more frequently it was military men, politicians, actors, theater and movie personages, and journalists who were born, while future scientists and physicians were born most rarely.

No one, as far as I know, has disputed the results of Gauquelin's studies from the technical standpoint, but from the conceptual standpoint they generated a very interesting interpretation.[5] Essentially it was as follows: Gauquelin's studies were undertaken on the basis of archival materials found in Europe (above all, the registrations of birth dates in church books), and a European usually knows what it means to be born at a time when

Mars is moving toward its culmination. Those around him know, and the "object" of the prediction himself knows at the time he chooses his profession. Gauquelin's experiment, accordingly, is not "pure" (no control group, etc.). But that is not the most important thing. This experiment reveals the mechanism of real coparticipation in the astrological tradition—a unique psychological and sociocultural effect of autosuggestion [*samonavedenie*].

The theoretical tools of astrology also promote the social and psychological autosuggestion of the "objects" of astrological prediction. The conceptual structures of astrology support these processes by virtue of their scientific status. In any event, this is how these structures are informed by a whole range of meaningful interpretive hypotheses of astrological theory. But the conceptual apparatus of astrology assumes a unique metaphorical character, which in turn facilitates the spread of astrological notions in everyday consciousness and thereby strengthens our capacity for autosuggestion.[6]

It must be said that there is nothing that fundamentally contraindicates science's being able to function in such socially and psychologically oriented structures, but if a certain balance breaks down in the course of this functioning, it will inevitably lead to its distortion. A recent striking example of this is so-called administrative science [*vedomstvennaia nauka*], which is ready to provide arguments in justification of anything at all and to "hook us up" to anything at all, unrelated to any tradition. A very shaky line exists here, and astrologers would do well to bear this in mind.

There is an astrological legend, which may be construed as a form of the methodological self-awareness of astrology. A certain Astrologer, a person devoted wholeheartedly to his profession, once did what generally speaking an astrologer should not do—he made a horoscope for himself and moreover wanted to know the time of his death. It turned out that the stars gave him a precise and unambiguous answer to his question. The astrologer spent the whole rest of the time left to him by the stars in checking and rechecking his calculations, clarifying his observations, and searching for inaccuracies. However, the stars were inexorable. And the Day arrived. But time passed, and death did not come. We can only guess what was taking place in his soul during this time, but the fact was that at the end of the day the Astrologer hung himself.

To the glory of his horoscope? Indisputably. But did he fall victim to his own belief and the psychological effect of autosuggestion in accordance with the principle of synergism, or were the stars inexorable? It is impossible to obtain an answer to this question. And, as long as it is impossible to do so, astrology remains in its own, so to speak, cultural niche, for it is capable of fulfilling quite effectively its main cultural function—it is capable of serving as one of the mechanisms of self-regulation of human activity.

Indeed, as far as its cultural functions are concerned, astrology does not differ from many other humanistic sciences, the essence of which amounts to social and psychological regulation by partaking in tradition. But just like these sciences, astrology is very sensitive to external sociocultural circumstances, which easily disrupt the inner balance of its opposing methodological orientations. It seems to me that this balance has at present been very gravely disrupted. The thing is that we have not been living by the stars for a long time now, and the rhythms of our life are set for the most part by the technological tasks of modern production, and we are very little capable of actually joining the astrological tradition.

Astrology today

The effect of astrological autosuggestion we are presently experiencing is fueled more by nostalgia for the stars than by the real state of affairs. And that of course prevents us from adequately partaking in the content of the millennial experience and penetrating into the rational structure of astrology to such a degree that the essence and the wisdom of the astrological tradition would be revealed to us. However, our nostalgia is quite sufficient to allow us to make these rational structures into the ideological expression of the unsatisfied needs fueling this nostalgia. Hence astrology acquires some of the features characteristic of ideology (of course not a social-class ideology, such as we are used to).

For the Russian reader, the term 'ideology' may evoke various associations. But in this particular case, let me remind the reader, we are speaking solely of the epistemological status of the corresponding conceptual structure, and hence it is here sufficient to point out that the rational structures in contemporary astrology are so blurred and so overtly the expression of precisely a sociocultural interest that they in fact are in opposition not to science but to other ideologies—religious, philosophical, so-called scientific ideology, and so forth. Contemporary astrology is characterized above all by the fact that it contains ecological values and also in the way it appropriates and represents these values. In the nineteenth century, progressive mankind dreamed of solving all problems by giving life a rhythm by a mechanical clock—and astrology then virtually disappeared. In the twentieth century, the idea of giving our lives a rhythm by the stars is very attractive to us—and therein, in my view, lies the essence of its renaissance today. Indeed, if an ideology helps us to survive, it has the right to existence. However, there is one circumstance here to which I should like to draw attention.

Contemporary astrology functions in our sociocultural environment like ideological structures, which in the consciousness of modern man appear in the form of scientifically grounded (historical, economic, political-scientific, ethnological, literary, etc.) knowledge. Like all of these sciences, astrology functions (depending on the level at which it operates) as an ideological or personal-psychological phenomenon, and just like all of these human sciences, astrology loses its capacity to fulfill its functions when it is reduced either to standard scientific investigation or (which is precisely the case of astrology) to overt divination. However, what we might call the negative sociocultural consequences of such deformations of astrology are not of equivalent value. Today we can hardly seriously be alarmed by astrology's claims to the status of a science; it is obvious today that its purpose is by no means cognitive, although astrology does fulfill its functions precisely by virtue of its scientific status. When astrological ideas are assimilated, say, by astrophysics or astrobiology, they lose their capacity to serve as a foundation for astrological "autosuggestion." And it is the reduction of astrology to astral divination severed from tradition that turns it into a powerful tool for manipulating consciousness in our present sociocultural context.

In itself, there is nothing "terrible" about the revival of astrology in our country—in time, in our country as well, it will obviously assume the place set aside for it in the spiritual life of the contemporary developed countries—that is, it will serve our contradictory desire to synchronize our lives in conformity with vital natural rhythms in an epoch of electronic clocks. It is not astrology in and of itself that harbors a danger. What is dangerous under conditions of an ideological vacuum is the inability to deal with this quite powerful sociocultural mechanism and especially the use of it for various sorts of political manipulations, reinforced, moreover, by the mass media. After all, it is often by no means clear in the name of what "stars" our TV astrologers today are auguring our political future.

Notes

1. There is a thirteenth constellation there as well—between Scorpio and Sagittarius, the Sun visits the constellation of the Serpent-Holder. But this constellation is not traditionally part of the Zodiac constellations, and astrologers rarely mention it (on very weakly rationalized grounds, one might add).

2. Aleister Crowley, *Astrologie. Archetypes de l'universe astrale selon la mythologie et*

les traditions occidentales (St. Jean de Braye, France, 1979). This edition is the latest French translation of the English editions (1947 and 1974) of Crowley's book.

3. Ibid., p. 59.

4. See Michel Gauquelin, *Les hommes et les astres* (Paris, 1960); *Cosmic Influence on Human Behavior* (London, 1974).

5. J.W. Kelly, "Astrology, Cosmobiology, and Humanistic Astrology," in *Philosophy of Science and the Occult*, ed. Patrick Grim (Albany, NY: State University of New York Press, 1982).

6. We are far from always even aware that astrology has given our everyday language such words as 'exaltation', 'depression', 'aspect', 'diametric opposites', 'retrograde', and 'influenza'.